An American Heritage

John T. Wayne

YBR PUBLISHING, LLC
Ridgeland, South Carolina

Jack Gannon – Co-Founder, Production Manager
Cyndi Williams-Barnier – Co-Founder, Production Editor
Bill Barnier – Senior Editor, Manager
Loreen Ridge-Husum – Art Director

ISBN-13: 979-8-9852082-7-6

AN AMERICAN HERITAGRE © Copyright 2023 John T. Wayne. All Rights Reserved and Preserved. No part of this book may be reproduced or transmitted in any form or by any means, electronic or mechanical, including photocopying, recording, or by information storage and retrieval systems, without written permission of the Publisher with exceptions as to brief quotes, references, articles, reviews, and certain other noncommercial uses permitted by copyright law.

Cover silhouette image source getdrawings.com

For Permission requests, write to:
YBR Publishing, LLC
PO Box 4904
Beaufort SC 29903-4904
contact@ybrpub.com

"The guy you see on the screen isn't really me. I'm Duke Morrison, and I never was and never will be a film personality like JOHN WAYNE. I know him well. I'm one of his closest students. I have to be. I made a living out of him."

~John Wayne

TABLE OF CONTENTS

PREFACE 1
CHAPTER 1 – GIVING CREDIT WHERE CREDIT IS DUE.......................... 7
CHAPTER 2 – TELLING THE TRUTH 11
CHAPTER 3 – DR. MORRISON'S OBITUARY 16
CHAPTER 4 – THE UNANSWERED QUESTION 24
CHAPTER 5 – A DESTINY TAKES HOLD 34
CHAPTER 6 – HOLD EVERYTHING, JOE JITSU...................................... 37
CHAPTER 7 – MY LIFE BEGINS 39
CHAPTER 8 – LIFE DOESN'T LET UP 41
CHAPTER 9 – NEW TREE BRANCHES 46
CHAPTER 10 – A TRUE AMERICAN 52
CHAPTER 11 – TURNING BACK THE CALENDAR 65
CHAPTER 12 – COINCIDENCE? PROBABLY NOT 67
CHAPTER 13 – JOHN T. WAYNE 69
CHAPTER 14 – THE SUMMARY 89
CHAPTER 15 – PROOF NOW FINDS ME 93
CHAPTER 16 – THE WILD GOOSE 98
CHAPTER 17 – JOHN WAYNE'S "SECOND SON" DIES 115
CHAPTER 18 – LIKE "GRANDPA", LIKE "GRANDSON" 121
EPILOGUE 122
POSTSCRIPT 124

ACKNOWLEDGEMENTS

Asa Hutchinson, Former Governor of Arkansas, for signing into law The True Grit Trail
Tom and Marilyn Shay, for their tireless promotion of The True Grit Trail
Indian Joe of West Memphis, Arkansas, for all the book signings he has arranged for me
Angela Courtney of Dumas, Arkansas, for setting my speaking engagements

Hopkins County Geological Society, Madisonville, Kentucky
    Theresa K Ray, Vice President and Librarian
    Steven D. Ray, Program Chair

And for their support of this book

Steve and Theresa Ray of Madisonville, Kentucky
Sylvia Evans of Harrisburg, Arkansas
Genealogical Society of Paragould, Arkansas
Museum of History in Fort Smith, Arkansas
U.S. Marshall Museum in Fort Smith, Arkansas
Hanging Judge Museum in Fort Smith, Arkansas

David DuPont and his wife Nancy
Jim Horton
Sheila Ragland
Warren Palmer
Steve Acree
Tammy Thompson
Tim Harris
Tom Brauns….

Roy Tudor
Hal Colson
Lowery Hesse

And all the family and friends who have supported me since this voyage of discovery began.

Finally, and especially, to the wonderful staff of YBR Publishing, LLC (Jack Gannon, Cyndi Williams-Barnier, Bill Barnier, Loreen Ridge-Husum) for bringing my voyage to reality.

To

*My father and mother,
Billy and Bonnie Hammock*

*My brothers,
John Andrew and William Eugene*

*My beautiful wife,
Donna*

For believing in me…

REVIEWS

Reviewed by Joe Wisinski for Readers' Favorite

People often told John T. Wayne, author of An American Heritage, that he looked a lot like the well-known actor John Wayne. Even Maureen O'Hara, who often worked in films with John Wayne, noticed the resemblance. John T. Wayne knew that merely resembling John Wayne didn't necessarily mean that they were related, but he was told about the similarity so many times that he decided to research the family history to try to find out if he was related to the actor. Even though his family was reluctant to provide him with the information he wanted, over the years he found overwhelming evidence that he was John Wayne's grandson. John T. Wayne was born Terry Wayne Hammock. He later changed his name legally to reflect his relationship with John Wayne. The book contains many photos of the author, his father, and John Wayne.

An American Heritage by John T. Wayne is a fascinating book. Although it's non-fiction, it reads like an intriguing novel written in the first person. It was especially interesting to read about how John T. Wayne compiled evidence, examining fact after fact that he dug up and fitting them together like a puzzle. He eventually determined that he was indeed John Wayne's grandson. I also admired John T. Wayne's persistence in discovering his heritage and possible relationship with John Wayne, even though some of what he found wasn't always positive or flattering to his extended family. This book may inspire some readers to research their genealogy, not because they're looking for famous ancestors, but because at some point most people want to know where they came from.

PREFACE

It has taken several years to piece together what information we have about the life-changing journey of one John Thomas Wayne. The information has come from many different sources and unexpected areas of the country, but it tells an incredible story like no other, a jigsaw puzzle of sorts. This memoir shows how it was possible for one young man, Billy Gene Hammock, born out of wedlock, to grow up, live his entire life, and never know his real father.

The trail is eighty-eight years long with many winding turns, the end of which we may never reach. It's a trail for three of Billy's sons, who grew up under the same hand-me-down shadow, unsolved, at least in his lifetime. I'm prepared for the story to outlast me, but I must tell you, I sure wasn't prepared for what I've learned so far. With that in mind, I believe you might have a hard time with some of what you're about to learn, I know my family does. Dad's family will not accept one piece of evidence in the matter, but that's their problem. Mark Twain once said, "No amount of evidence will ever persuade an idiot."

This book is for the other folks; those who have an open mind and have the capacity to deduce and reason for themselves. It's for the American people who have never heard of John Wayne's second child. For that matter, it's for the whole world. I'm not seeking damages nor money from the family. It's quite possible The Duke's family found out much like I did. They had nothing to do with what happened eighty-eight years ago, just like me; none of us were born yet. When did they learn about another possible brother? I have no idea, but some in The Duke's family must know about it. I'm certain they hope this book never reaches your eyes; my hope is that it does.

All I ever wanted to do was be a good western author, like Louis L'Amour or Zane Grey. But my past, or should I say my lack of a past, or any family history beyond that of my father, eventually caught up with me. It came back to haunt me, as they say. I never knew who my grandfather was, never heard his name spoken. That's a strange way to grow up. Such things trouble a young man's soul; such circumstances produce an unknown, a void in life which, in the end, causes a boy to wonder into adulthood. Then one day the boy becomes a man, then a mature man in his mid-fifties with no answers. My father never got any of these answers, he never looked beyond the surface. In truth, I don't think he wanted to, knowing he was lied to by his family was hard enough.

The truth I have to tell is as strange as anything you will find in the Bible. It began in Winterset, Iowa and Hollywood, USA. By design, there is more than one generation involved. The impact upon lives, many years after The Duke departed this world, is my story. It is a truthful account of what happened and how John Wayne likely had more children than any one person ever knew.

The Author at John Wayne birthplace, Winterset, Iowa

Over the last decade I've been hearing things such as "Why did you stake your claim as The Duke's grandson?", "Are you kin to John Wayne?", "Are you sure you're

The Duke's grandson?", "You look so much like him.", "I want to know what the lineage is!", "Who was your father?", "Are you really sure about all of this?" More than anything, this has led me to pen my answers to all those questions, and possibly more.

The Author

Today there is no doubt, just as there was no doubt when I staked my claim. The stacks of evidence, legal documents, historical facts, first-person affirmations from folks who knew The Duke, and my DNA analysis indicating nearly identical geographical heritage, all reinforce my claim.

Understandably, folks expect me to be like The Duke. I may be a chip off the old block, but I'm not The Duke. We're so much alike in beliefs and attitude that it's scary, especially when you realize I never met my grandfather. I inherited my attitude from my father, who also never knew The Duke, who I posit is his real father. All he knew was he'd been lied to by his own family. Honestly, I think the only reason he visited his family at times was in the hope that someday his mother might slip up and reveal the big family secret. My father died never knowing his rightful heritage. So, this book is justice: justice for a man who never knew his father, and justice for three sons who never heard the name of their grandfather spoken.

Looks alone don't make me John Wayne's grandson. My dad was the spitting image of John, though he was crippled and never gave off that "he-man" aura. Now there is my son Ryan, who also looks just like The Duke. So, three generations of family, all looking like The Duke, makes an overly compelling case. You would be right to say that just because we all resemble The Duke, doesn't make us family. But without question, we now have four generations, five if you include Clyde Morrison, The Duke's father, with the same genes, characteristics, and that look! The hidden truth of the eighty-eight-year mystery is no longer aimed at this western author but has grown to include most of the men in my family, as well as a new generation, my grandchildren. You see where this is headed? How many generations must we prove?

When you're born, you don't get to pick your own family. You're never assured of pleasantries in life, and you play the cards you're dealt. Not the ones you wish you had, nor those of someone else. I believe we are placed upon our life's path long before we're ever born. Many things that happened before I was born brought me to this exact point in my life today. Had we been told who our grandfather was when we were just young boys, I believe there would be no questions now. Perhaps life would have been different. We'll never know.

As written in Jeremiah 1: 1- " Before I formed you in the womb I knew you, before you were born, I set you apart."

Many screen actors in the early years of cinema were employees of the movie studios. Actors' skills and personalities were matched with movie rolls, then movies were written for those most successful. John Wayne (born Marion Robert Morrison, then Marion Michael Morrison) was an exceptional actor whose movie persona became his own iconic translation as to what it meant to be an American in the 20th century. His success came at a time when America and the world needed heroes and role models. But many celebrities were not saints. They had lives off the movie sets and made mistakes, just as you and I can make. John Wayne had children long before he became the iconic actor who we all know and love.

This book details my journey to seek the truth concerning my lost family heritage, the one that was hidden when my father was born. It is my quest to recover my family's true AMERICAN HERITAGE. I call it that because, to my knowledge and in my opinion, there was no bigger icon in the movie industry than John Wayne and no more celebrated American. I believe in God with all my heart, as I believe did my grandfather.

It is my hope that you will get to know Terry Wayne Hammock for who I was, born into circumstances beyond his control, and John T. Wayne for who I am now, patriot and United States Marine who can still shoot Expert at five-hundred yards.

A HELPING HAND

There is no doubt about the honorable heritage of the U.S. Marshals. John Wayne made a good one in the movies. A portion of the proceeds from this book will help fund the new UNITED STATES MARSHALS MUSEUM (usmmuseum.org) recently built-in downtown Fort Smith, Arkansas on the banks of the Arkansas River. The building is shaped like a star for good reason.

Another portion of the proceeds will also contribute to the TRUE GRIT TRAIL, from the City of Dardanelle in Yell County to Fort Smith, Arkansas. The overall wellbeing of our TRUE GRIT heritage in Arkansas is a priority for me. We christened the Trail using our classic nineteen-sixty Thunderbird, and Dan Eoff's 1927 Ford, along with the help from the Tri County Cruisers and many others, on August 23, 2020. We began a tradition of driving the Trail in classic automobiles, which I will do for the rest of my life, however long that is. All classic American automobiles are welcome on future trail drives. My upcoming U.S. Marshal book series will also support these great segments of our AMERICAN HERITAGE. If you ever want to do something different, join us in Dardanelle in Yell County, Arkansas, the home of Mattie Ross.

The True Grit Thunderbird

John T's Thunderbird – True Grit Trail

We continue to make upgrades to the Thunderbird each year (strictly Ford), it's a stick shift car making it one very rare Thunderbird. But this car also belongs to me, who stands six feet four inches. It isn't an easy thing for me to climb into and out of or drive this car. There's no power steering, no power brakes, no air conditioning, nor any other bells and whistles. That, along with a manual transmission, makes the car a handful to drive. It takes a little grit to handle this one, and that's the way I like it. That, and being known as the TRUE GRIT Thunderbird, makes this classic Thunderbird even more special for me as I continue to put my mark on the car, always improving when time allows. I do most of the work myself at home in my own shop when I'm not working on my next book.

CHAPTER 1
GIVING CREDIT WHERE CREDIT IS DUE

I'm often asked if I'm kin to John Wayne. The resemblance does seem uncanny, especially as I've gotten older. In my own defense, I wasn't sure in the beginning. Was it possible that I had any tie to one of the biggest movie actors to ever have a star on the Hollywood Walk of Fame? After seventy-five years is it possible to seek the answer to the nagging question of my heritage? I mean, come on; nobody in his right mind thinks he's John Wayne's grandson when no one ever alluded to that possibility in fifty-plus years. Yet, something always happened to soften those doubts, or another piece of information or meeting someone at the right time. Eventually, after having an almost week-long argument with the Lord, I gathered my thoughts and memories and started to investigate my father's dead-end heritage. I really had no idea where to look. "Lord, I'm going to need a little help here, because I don't have a clue where to begin!" Suddenly, answers began arriving. Many things had to happen first, and there would be people who would not take kindly to me staking any claim where The Duke is concerned. But today I'm finally resolved to the fact that I truly am John Thomas Wayne, I believe I am the biological grandson of John Wayne. I don't make such a claim lightly, and I don't expect anyone to just take it for granted. In fact, I welcome a real honest-to-goodness investigation into the facts presented here.

The Author and his wife, Donna

Donna, my wife and best friend for more than thirty years, has always been there for me. She's been witness to all of this. Does anyone who knows her think for one minute that if I was making all of this up that she'd still be with me? Not likely! Sure, we've had our tough spots, usually having to do with my inability to hold a job. I'd walk away from a good job if things got too stupid. You know who they are, the "little big men" who had to take down the big guy to prove their worth. They like to see just how far they can push their employees. But I'm a large guy and I can be just as intimidating. I'm intelligent as well, and I don't cotton to condescension just because I'm tall and carry myself well, (something I learned in the Marines). John Wayne only played a Marine; but I am one, and life has taught me how to fight.

The Author (L) and Sgt. McCarthy, Flight Line, 29 Palms

Donna always encouraged me to take the next step up. Were it not for her love and understanding, that step could have easily been a step down. Sometimes, I wondered what she saw in me. There were times I didn't see much there, whatever it was. Life is like that for anyone and everyone. There are times when others see the beauty and the wonder in you when you yourself haven't got a clue. When I thought I'd ruined our lives, she still believed in me, never allowing me to quit or give up. She wouldn't hear of it.

One thing that always nagged at me, however, was the thought that I didn't know my family heritage. It was quite literally missing, with no answers from Mom, Dad, or Granny, who as co-conspirator most certainly should know. It became a troublesome thing at times, perhaps a bit unfair to Donna. My wife, together with my Aunt Rose and my mother Bonnie, never doubted me. They didn't argue with me, even when they didn't understand. They encouraged me to go find something else. These three women have seen me destroyed more than once and took the time to tell me there was enough of me left to save. They gave me the benefit of the doubt, along with their love and devotion.

Like my father, I would have died without knowing my true family heritage had they not insisted I never give up or quit. I think what happened lends itself to the idea that most women are the backbone of American society, and they know their place even if we don't. If a man is having trouble, they are great at setting him straight, holding him up and telling him to get back in the ring. I know this from my own experience. I'd like to mention my Aunt Vivian here, too. She was really my great aunt, but I never heard her say a bad word about anyone. In fact, if you ever said something bad about someone in front of her, she'd have such a reaction as to let you know that she did not approve of your comment or anything about it by proclaiming, "Not in my house!" She wouldn't think of letting any evil spirit in the door. She understood that when a man goes out into the world, sometimes all he's dealing with is evil of one kind or another and it might still be on his shoulder when he came home in the evening. She never gave place to such a thing. I love my Aunt Vivian to this day.

CHAPTER 2
TELLING THE TRUTH

John Wayne once said; "If I offend you, you can be damn sure I intended to do it." This came as a direct result of The Duke's upbringing, because his father, Clyde Morrison, taught him never to offend anyone unintentionally. Oh, how I wish I could have learned that art form! All *I* have to do is open my mouth and someone gets offended! My point is: there are those who will be offended because I took the time to write this book. I haven't quite the upbringing my grandfather had, and from time-to-time such offenses happen quite unintentionally. But just so you know, every word in this book is intentional. You see, this author wants the heritage he was denied, the family heritage my father never knew existed. But the family tree was severed with my father, a tree branch potentially from the mighty John Wayne oak which the rest of the family hangs on to. I want that tree limb put back into place. I don't think that's asking too much considering the facts I have uncovered in the past twelve years.

It is my opinion that for years the publishing and media business has been gradually moving away from the need to seek and print the truth. Profits from delivering entertainment in books, newspapers and periodicals has become the governing rule. That, and telling people what they want to hear, tossing the truth overboard like a dead sailor at sea in favor of the almighty dollar.

But what if my account meets the truth requirement by telling the truth, the whole truth, and nothing but the truth? That would be different, wouldn't it? I have many books in my personal library written in the 1800s and early 1900s. Back then you had to write the truth, and it had to pass muster as the truth before the work was released, unless it was a fictional novel. No misleading statements, content or lies made it into print unless it was a declared work of fiction. All of that changed with the new age of motion pictures, television, and radio. Truth is no longer what it once was, yet truth means everything to me, because of the deceptions in my family. The only reason the lie came undone is because I didn't believe family lies anymore. I'd met too many people who made me question my own sanity: "Do you know who you look like?" Sometimes, I get inundated with questions like this all day long.

For the rest of my life people will be asking me questions and filling in more pieces of my heritage puzzle. Yet the truth is what we all want, and this memoir is a big dose of truth because nothing else is acceptable. This book is going to be examined front to back looking for any kind of a misplaced idea or mistake, especially something that isn't true. No, although I am a writer at heart and capable of writing a good fictional story, I hope you will agree, nothing in this book can be made up.

As my life story evolved, it was difficult to decide where to begin. So much has happened and continues to happen in my life that my head starts spinning sometimes. Once this story is told, no doubt there will be even more to learn, because there is more out there, and I hope it all comes during the rest of my lifetime.

The facts I'm going to share with you are directly related to my father and his origins, so it becomes necessary to place a little background on your plate.

We learned The Duke was a breeder of Hereford cattle, and besides his ranch in Arizona he kept cattle in Illinois, Kentucky, Texas, and Oklahoma. There were a few south of the border, as well. Also, Mr. Walter Ruby of Kentucky was a premier breeder of Herefords for forty years and was a life-long friend of The Duke. He was also Catholic and a 32nd-degree Mason. His breeding techniques were sought after by many cattlemen, but The Duke became his close friend and confidant, picking his brain many times. They kept, bought, and sold cattle together for years. Ruby, the president of Kentucky State Bank, bought a house in Newport Beach, not realizing it wouldn't get him any more precious time with The Duke, who continued making movies.

However, if you read much about John Wayne, his only cattle partner ever mentioned was Louis Johnson in Arizona. Yet he had many partners and associates in the cattle business, not just Louis Johnson, as we had been led to believe. Whenever The Duke visited Walter, it was not uncommon for them to sit on the front porch at the house and drink, sometimes for a week or more. Since John Wayne was known to be a lady's man, Walter tried to keep up. As you can see, it almost got him killed.

The Messenger (Madisonville, Kentucky)
03 Aug 1966, Wed
Page 1

Charged In Shooting Spree
Mrs. Ruby Is Released From Jail On Bond

Mrs. Georgia Ruby, charged in Hopkins County Court with maliciously shooting without wounding, with intent to kill Monday after taking shots at her husband, Walter Ruby, and two Madisonville policemen in a two and one-half hour shooting spree at the Ruby home Sunday night, has been released from county jail on a $2,000 appearance bond and a $5,000 peace bond, both signed by Walter Ruby.

At noon today Mrs. Ruby had not appeared in county court yet. County Judge Hubert Reid has a certificate signed by a local physician stating that Mrs. Ruby is unable to appear in court. The doctor's statement was given as the reason for not having arraigned Mrs. Ruby yet.

She was arrested shortly before midnight Sunday, on a complaint signed by Madisonville Patrolman Harold Ford, when 13 local law enforcement officers were required to make the arrest.

Mrs. Ruby, using a .45 caliber gold plated, pearl handled Colt revolver and a 30.30 Winchester saddle carbine, allegedly took shots at Madisonville Police Captain Bob Burton, Patrolman Ford, and her husband, Walter Ruby. She was arrested after being routed from a hiding place, in some shrubbery near the Ruby home, by two tear gas grenades.

Meanwhile, in a suit filed in the office of Hopkins Circuit Court Clerk Wallace Kingten Ruby is seeking a divorce from Georgia Ruby.

In the complaint, filed by Madisonville Attorney Richard Frymire, Ruby charges cruel and inhuman treatment, stating that he has "suffered such cruel beatings and injuries and attempts at injury at the hands of his wife so as to indicate an outrageous temper in the defendant and if the parties continue to live together there is probable danger to his life or of great bodily injury."

Attorney Frymire is also acting as Mrs. Ruby's counsel in the county court shooting charge. Mrs. Ruby, however, was expected to appear in county court later today.

©1966 The Messenger, Ancestry.com source

Ruby was generous, loyal friend

BY SAMANTHA CARVER
Messenger Staff Writer
scarver@the-messenger.com

WEDNESDAY, FEBRUARY 2, 2000

Prominent Madisonville businessman Walter J. Ruby Jr. died Tuesday at the age of 80.

Ruby, retired director of Kentucky Bank and Trust Company and Bank One, cattle breeder and farmer, is a longtime resident of Madisonville.

Ruby

He lived in the home where he was born on Evergreen Hill Farms at 1201 East Center Street for the majority of his life.

"Walter was my friend, and I will miss him," said Judge-Executive Dick Frymire of Madisonville. "He was one of the very interesting citizens of Madisonville and Hopkins County."

Frymire said Ruby was a good friend to all those who knew him.

"He had friends from Kentucky to California," he said.

FRIEND
(Continued from A1)

was faithful to his friends."

The son of Walter J. Ruby and Anna Grace Connor Ruby of Madisonville, and the stepson of Charles Jennings of New Castle, Ind., he was born Oct. 12, 1919.

His prize-winning registered Hereford cattle were shown throughout the United States until they were dispersed in 1982.

For 40 years, he was nationally known for his selective breeding techniques and his overall methods of agriculture.

He actively participated in programs to improve the nutrition and maintenance of feeder cattle.

Ruby was a member of the American Hereford Association and the Kentucky Hereford Association, and served on the Committee of National Cattlemen's Association for many years.

He enjoyed woodworking, building model boats, collecting antique automobiles and fishing throughout North America.

"He always had a project to do," said Dr. Jim Donley of Madisonville. "He was very good in photography and building models. He was also a man who gave unselfishly of himself in many ways."

Donley agreed with Frymire that Ruby gave very willingly of himself as a friend, and even had friends as well known as movie star John Wayne.

"They raised Hereford cattle together, and were very good buddies," Donley said.

While Ruby kept to himself generally, Donley called him a true gentleman.

"He called everyone he cared about 'Dearheart' and always kissed women's hands," he said. "He was a good friend of mine, and I will sorely miss him."

Donley said many people did not realize how generous Ruby actually was to the community.

"He came into my office one day and gave me a check for $3,000, and he said to donate it to whoever I thought needed it, but never to tell them where I got the money," Donley said. "He will be missed more than some people realize because of the things he did in the background."

Ruby is preceded in death by his wife, Helen Marie Ruby in 1996.

Survivors include three sons, Walter, Turner and Laurel Ruby of Indianapolis, Ind.; a daughter, Ann Connor Ruby Heim of Orlando, Fla.; a step-daughter, Pamela White of Sacramento, Calif.; three step-sons, Duncan Harding of Woodland Park, Colo., Terry Harding of Atlanta, Ga., and Chris Northam of Paris, Tenn.; and several grandchildren and great-grandchildren.

He is also survived by his long-time friend and general manager Jay B. Higgins.

Funeral arrangements are being handled by Barnett-Strother Funeral Home. Both viewing and services will be held at Ruby's residence at 1201 East Center Street with entombment to follow in Odd Fellows Cemetery at the family mausoleum.

The viewing will be from 4 p.m. to 7 p.m. Thursday, and there will be a private service.

Pallbearers will be Dick Frymire, Edwin Ruby, Larry Alexander, Jay Higgins, Chris Northam and Jim Donley. Honorary pallbearers will be O.T. Rudd and L.W. Simpson.

Memorial contributions may take the form of donations to St. Mary's Episcopal Church.

Photo ©2000 The Messenger, Ancestry.com source

    Another mystery is the discovery of Dr. John C. Morrison. Dr. Morrison was seemingly well-liked, but we have found almost no records of him beyond his obituary. None of his records were archived, nor were his journals. It was commonplace for educated people to keep journals, so it is reasonable to assume that the good doctor kept some as well. He lived in a small town, probably with only one physician, and was the replacement for the ageing Dr. Baker, M.D.

    So, where are his journals, or the records of his medical practice? This makes our records search a difficult matter, though we finally stumbled across just what we needed. I will tie this all together for you later, but is it too far-fetched to consider that the records and journals have been hidden or destroyed to cover up my father's birth? Like Ruby, Dr. Morrison was also a 32nd-degree Mason. Dr. Morrison was president of the Kentucky Medical Association while Ruby was head of Kentucky State Bank. Imagine the reputations they had before John Wayne became an American Icon. By these men helping him accomplish his ultimate station in life, imagine their reputations after.

CHAPTER 3
DR. MORRISON'S OBITUARY

When looking back over the last twelve years of my life and how things unfolded, I am amazed; I never saw any of it coming. The first fifty years of my life as Terry Wayne Hammock came and went without me ever knowing who my maternal grandfather was. I was cruising along, minding my own affairs, because I figured out long ago, no one in my family was ever going to tell me one little piece of truth about my heritage. That's a strange circumstance, but as it turns out it was necessary. Had anyone told me who my grandfather was, that he died and was gone, I would have accepted matters and been fine with it. But no one ever told us anything; not my mother, my father, my grandmother, aunts, uncles, no one said a word. Why couldn't anyone in my father's family tell me something? It was because no one knew anything except my grandmother, and for some reason she never offered up the truth. She never told us a lie, but she also wouldn't give us any answers. She simply said nothing to my father or me and took that one family secret to her grave. I'm certain, as she was a godly woman late in life, she had everything reconciled with the good Lord. I cannot conceive of her handling things in any other way. She was good at being a grandmother, a great-grandmother, and great-great-grandmother to myriad numbers of children…we have a big family!

She was born Lela Pearl Clements, then took on her married name: Gordon. The rest of her children took the name Gordon, but not my dad. It's important to note that he believed his given name was Clements, which made him the odd ball out. The fact he had Spina-Bifida when he was born also placed him in the position of being estranged.

The new husband wanted nothing to do with my father, so Grandma Clements stepped in and continued the lie by claiming to be Billy Gene Clements' mother, and Lela Pearl Clements was Dad's sister. I think it's important to say that when you begin a family lie, it takes more lies to cover it up and keep it going. Sometimes those lies spread to include the entire family. But, as with all lies at some point the truth is going to come to the surface. My father, Billy Gene Hammock, was my Granny's first-born son. Thinking they were protecting him, they were actually hurting him beyond reason. What they were really protecting were the reputations of a beautiful young woman and the wholesome image (and profits) of a rising Hollywood star.

Before we forget about Doctors Morrison and Baker, let's clear the air a bit. Dr. Baker moved his practice to Hickman, Kentucky around 1897 and was already a practicing physician. He and his wife soon after settled into small town life. He was the doctor in Hickman for twenty-five or thirty years before easing into retirement. At about 1921 Dr. Morrison came to town and took over as the area's lead physician. He bought a home on top of the bluff overlooking the Mississippi River. He had a young family and they also settled into small town life. But this is where I believe the opportunity to hide a mistake met with the means to do just that.

If Dr. Morrison delivered all of Granny's children, as the family claimed, why is my father's birth certificate dated 1935 signed by Dr. Baker? Truth be known, it isn't. Let's look at this closely because nothing on this certificate adds up.

AN AMERICAN HERITAGE

The Author's Father's Birth Certificate

If one looks carefully at the handwriting, one will note that it is all intentionally perfect, not the normal doctor scribble offered during a routine day. Every letter was written intentionally and perfectly. But the thing that raised my eyebrow was all three signatures on this certificate appear to be written by the same person; not Granny, not Victor Hammock and not even Dr. J.T. Baker, which I will prove in a moment. Clearly this is a forgery!

For comparison, we have the death certificate of James Wynegar Hammock signed by Dr. Morrison during a routine day. The handwriting on my father's birth certificate is in the same hand as the person who filled out this death certificate about eighteen years later. You can see a small difference in the handwriting, but the main difference is the person who did this was doing so as a routine part of their day, not like my father's birth certificate! It's clearly the same person, and this person worked for Dr. Morrison. Why did this same person sign for Doctor J. T. Baker on my father's birth certificate? Doctor Baker had already retired. There's something fishy going on here.

Why didn't Dr. Morrison want his signature on my father's birth certificate? Why resort to forgery? Why would a nurse go along with something so devious? That's something to think about, but as you can see in the next document, the signature on my father's birth certificate clearly is not that of J. T. Baker, M.D. The handwriting of doctors is not something that gets better as they get older. It generally deteriorates into illegible scribble and Baker would have been nearing the age of ninety-three at the time of my father's birth. I've never heard of a ninety-year-old retired doctor handling a birth for anyone.

Dr. Baker was born June 21st, 1843. One would have to believe that he was still a practicing physician in his nineties in 1935 for him to have delivered my father. Therefore, I do not believe Dr. Baker delivered my father. Dr. Baker's ancestry leads directly to William Penn, the founder of Philadelphia.

You may be asking yourself right about now: what has the name Hammock got to do with Duke Morrison or John Wayne? If you were going to bury someone's identity so he could never be found as a relative, why would you use the name Wayne, Morrison or anything to do with The Duke? I believe you wouldn't! Especially if you are in fact the delivery physician John C. Morrison, M.D., head of the Kentucky Medical Association, and you know what happened at your home in your town of Hickman, Kentucky. You'd absolutely want that kind of scandal buried deep! You're a 32nd-degree Mason, the young man responsible was a distant relative, but a relative nevertheless, and an up-and-coming

Mason. It wasn't just Duke Morrison's reputation on the line here. Dr. John C. Morrison's reputation, all of it, was on the line as well.

There is plenty here to examine and study on these three certificates alone, but we're going to move on. There is so much more to this story, and I don't want to get hung up on the endless possibilities.

The Paducah Sun (Paducah, Kentucky)
11 Jun 1964, Thu
Page 26

Hickman Doctor Of 43 Years Dies

HICKMAN, Ky., June 10 — Dr. John Coulter Morrison, 80, a physician here for 43 years, died at 3:30 a.m. Wednesday at Baptist Hospital in Memphis.

A past president of the Kentucky Medical Association, Dr. Morrison had practiced until last week, when he became ill.

He was taken to the Memphis Hospital, where he underwent surgery last Sunday.

A graduate of the Vanderbilt University Medical School, class of 1906, Dr. Morrison came to Hickman in 1921. He was a native of Clarksville, Tenn.

He was a member of First Methodist Church here and had served on its Board of Stewards. He was a 32nd Degree Mason.

For 40 years he was a member of the Fulton County Board of Health and resigned only recently.

Surviving are his wife, Mrs. Bess Shelton Morrison; a daughter, Mrs. Warwick Hale of Hickman; a son, John William Morrison of Union City, Tenn., eight grandchildren and one great-grandchild.

Funeral services were held at 4 p.m. today at First Methodist Church, the Rev. King Dickerson and the Rev. Lowell Council of Covington, Tenn. officiating.

Burial was in Hickman City Cemetery.

Members of the medical staffs of Obion County Hospital in Union City and Fuller-Gilliam Hospital in Mayfield will be honorary pallbearers.

©1964 The Paducah Sun

CHAPTER 4
THE UNANSWERED QUESTION

As kids, when we asked about our grandfather, we were told; "Go play, it's none of your business." Neither I, nor my brothers, give up that easy. While I played with my brothers and cousins, the question kept ringing in my head. I tried Grandma, Grandpa Gordon, and my own mother, whose maiden name was Moore, and my father, who was a Hammock even though his brother and sisters were all Gordons. All I ever got was "It's none of your business, go play." WHY? The three of us boys wondered where the name "Hammock" came from.

As a boy I was a bit naïve and quiet; probably the best description "timid" comes to mind. The world around me always seemed to be moving under my feet. As a family, we didn't stay in one place too long. The longest we stayed anywhere was two years, because Dad's job situation was always changing. One year I went to four different schools! It's hard to get your feet set under you when you're constantly the new kid in school. Every time you check into a new class the entire focus is on a subject your previous school hadn't gotten to yet or something you knew nothing about. I was there to learn, but I was just thrown into the mix and had to figure out a way to sort it out. By the time I managed to do that, I usually only had bits and pieces of the overall picture I was supposed to receive. There were a few positives: I learned how to meet folks and there were Civil War Battlefields all over Missouri, and I learned about most of them.

When we were young boys, the three of us could have been the stars of "The Good, The Bad and The Ugly"! We each packed a pair of six shooters and in our minds, we were top dogs in the old west. We had cowboy boots, hats and a never-ending supply of imaginary ammo. We even had ropes. There wasn't a villain who could trick us, outdraw us or get away from us. We were that good. We were what I consider single digit Pistoleros.

My older brother John never had problems making friends or fending for himself. I guess that's part of being the oldest. He always made the right friends at the drop of a hat. He became an engineer with a degree from LSU putting himself through school while working on oil rigs in the Gulf of Mexico. (It seems I owe him at least one classic Mustang.) He was "The Duke" in our bunch growing up. We didn't look up to John Wayne; we looked up to our brother John Andrew Hammock! He always had the right answer and wasn't opposed to watching out for or coaching his younger brothers. Dad just couldn't.

When I was in the fourth grade in Independence, Missouri, the school bully, Ricky, took a liking to picking on me. I was quiet and withdrawn, and he was the school bully who was supposed to be in the seventh grade, but he was stuck in fourth grade for the third time. To this day I still tote the pencil lead in my knee where he stabbed me.

One day I caught my brother in the hallway, and I told him Ricky was going to beat me up on my way home from school. "No, he isn't," was his calm reply. "You meet me and Danny right here when school lets out and we'll walk you home."

The Author's brothers and cousins

    I met them as planned and we began the trek home. Just as we cleared the fenced walkway Ricky jumped out from behind some bushes saying, "Now you're gonna get a whoopin'." His mistake was *talking* when he should have been *doing*. My brother leveled him with three of the quickest jabs I ever saw a man or boy throw, then he jumped on top of the boy and went to wailing on him. With each punch he told Ricky he would get much worse if he ever bothered me again. Ricky was just flapping his hands around haplessly trying to avoid the next punch to his face.

    When we got home my brother had worn his knuckles raw from boxing the boy's jaw. I knew my brother had been in boxing since the second grade, but I had no idea how it helped one's fighting ability, until then. The next day at school it looked like Ricky had had a run-in with a freight train, but he never bothered me again. In fact, we became friends until the Hammock family moved once again. The construction of the Blue Ridge Mall was complete, and Dad was needed elsewhere. Maybe it was the bank, I really don't remember.

I was the shy beanpole in the family, but I never had any trouble cleaning the scraps off the dining room table. Dad used to say I would eat the family out of house and home, but I was growing so tall so fast, food never stuck with me long.

The cloud of family mystery clung to us wherever we went. Imagine living your life with the resolve that you'll never know the name of your grandfather. For whatever reason, it was Top Secret information we couldn't have. I wondered if he was a bank robber, a killer locked up for life, or some evil minion of the Devil himself. Eventually you give up and go on with your life, which is what my brothers and I did in the mid-seventies. One went to college and the other two of us joined the United States Marine Corps. We sure weren't going to cry over "spilled milk", as the family called it. I was sworn into the Corps in July 1976 and never looked back. Without the answers we deserved, the game of life was set for me.

```
UNITED STATES MARINE CORPS
    2nd Battalion, 9th Marines
3d Marine Division,(-)(Rein), FMF
     FPO San Francisco 96602
```

5 May 1977

Dear Mrs. HAMMOCK,

I am most pleased to inform you that your son has recently been promoted to Private First Class.

It was indeed a source of satisfaction for me to recognize the abilities and efforts of such a fine young man. He is a hard worker and I hope that there will be many more promotions for him during his service as a Marine.

While I recognize that you undoubtedly miss Terry during this overseas assignment, I hope that the hardship is lessened by your knowledge of his success in the Corps.

Sincerely yours,

JOHN T. GARCIA
Lieutenant Colonel, U. S. Marine Corps
Commanding

I'll admit I got into trouble in the Marine Corps a few times. The first problem I never understood, though eventually I figured out what happened. A Marine is supposed to have honor, and I soon found out the hard way that isn't always the case.

A Staff Sergeant friend of mine was sent to Hawaii for a few years from Camp Pendleton. He left a light blue four-speed '67 SS396 Chevelle with me to sell for $1000. I had two Chevelles of my own, a '68 SS396 Convertible, a red and black hardtop along with a V-8 Vega. But at twenty-three years old I'd never sold anything.

The Staff Sergeant left the car and the signed title with me. Another Marine said he wanted it and gave me $200 down with a promise to pay the rest. Two weeks later he said he needed the title so he could get it registered and borrow the rest of the money from the credit union. As you can guess, my lack of experience bit me in the rear real hard. As a result, I was busted back to an E-3 for cheating the Staff Sergeant and I never got the chance to offer an explanation. That lesson left a bitter taste. I don't mind getting busted for something if I deserve it, but I didn't cheat anyone. I trusted that Marine and he cheated ME, twice! That's why I now say, "Revenge is the lowest form of human behavior on the planet. It always hurts the wrong people."

Another incident at Camp Pendleton added insult to injury. I was robbed at gunpoint by three Marines from New York. Having a gun shoved to the back of my head while they went through my wallet certainly has a way of adjusting one's view of folks from the Big Apple.

"Where's your money?" they demanded. "It's payday!"

Out of fear of becoming a corpse right then, I told the truth, "My check is under my pillow in my room. I haven't cashed it yet."

It was Friday night and I guess they thought I should have several hundred dollars on me, but all I had was a $20 dollar bill. They continued to make me look at the ground with steady pressure from their gun on the back of my head. I guess they figured there was better pickings elsewhere because they told me to run away, not to look back or it would be the last thing I did. Well, I ran alright; straight to the MP station two blocks away to report what happened. That was the fastest I ever ran in my life.

Those thieves were so offended that all I had in my wallet was money left over from my last check, I was sure they were going to shoot me anyway. I've never been to New York for a visit or to see anything there. Imagine that!

At the age of twenty I was stationed at Camp Pendleton and still learning how much I didn't know about people and life in general. My unit had just returned from sunny Twenty-Nine Palms after a three-month deployment for desert training, arriving on a frigid day in mid-February. Because of outstanding service, I had been recently promoted, so the CO put me in charge of the guard detail so I could bask in my success. All but a few of the privates assigned to me got the weekend off, but someone had to guard the equipment from the extreme cold.

The nights were bitterly cold, but we made it through the weekend until late Sunday night / early Monday morning when the only stove we had for heat ran out of diesel fuel. Private Davenport was inside when it died out so yours truly sent him to find a can of diesel. Anything labeled "diesel" on the back of a vehicle would suffice. That's exactly what he returned with, but when I tipped the can up to fill the still hot stove, we discovered the hard way it wasn't diesel fuel, it was gasoline. The fumes ignited in my face. I set the can down as easily as possible under the circumstances, but the tall lanky me wasn't coordinated enough to remain calm while my face burned. I turned to run out the door, tripped over the can I'd placed at my feet, landing in the spilled fuel which lit me up like Johnny Storm!

Private Davenport grabbed me by the arm as I tried to get up, but I was on fire from head to toe. I couldn't see where I was going. Once we made it out the door I dropped to the ground and rolled to snuff out the flames, just in time for my guard detail to appear. They used their field jackets to finish the job. I ordered one of them to run to the nearest telephone and call the Fire Department. By then it was about four in the morning so there wasn't much else to do but stand there and watch the building burn.

As the Fire Department put out the last of the flames just after sunrise the Fire Captain came over to me with a serious look on his face. "Marine, you need to take yourself to the hospital. That's an order!"

Commandeering a nearby Jeep, which would do nicely, I later learned it was the same jeep Davenport got the fuel can from. Once seated, I looked in the rear-view mirror and was shocked to see a total stranger. It scared the hell out of me. I couldn't feel the pain because it was cold. I was not only burned but nearly frozen by the open-air ride by the time I got myself to the Camp Pendleton Emergency Room. I also stank of gasoline.

Those doctors and nurses scrubbed my face for at least three hours, and got me out of my stinking clothes, which went straight into a trash bag, then outside. All I got to keep was my wallet. I'm quite certain they had no trouble incinerating them as they were completely saturated in gasoline. From the ER I was given a room on the seventh floor with a view of most of Camp Pendleton and a chance to rest, or so I thought. When my Navy doctor came to see me, he told me I would be in the hospital for about six or seven weeks. He explained that as a burn victim my life would probably change dramatically.

"You need to roll over on your side and let my nurse give you a shot. It's Morphine, a narcotic, so it's going to hurt going in." At this point the nurse took over. I've since learned that doctors don't want to look at your behind, but a nurse? Why, they don't mind at all! I think it may be their favorite part of the anatomy. I've had so many shots there; my right-side buttock still hurts in my old age. That's still their favorite spot forty years later.

Once the doctor mentioned Morphine, all I could think of was the time my mother worked at a hospital years earlier and some fellow was so high on Morphine he jumped to his death from the seventh-floor window. For several hours I struggled with thoughts I can't explain even today. My biggest fear was repeating the mistake that poor unfortunate fellow made years before. Then the pain, stress, fear, and morphine delivered me to a place called twenty-four hours of oblivion.

When I came to, my roommate and good friend Sgt. Kurt McCarthy was by my side. "I've been worried about you," he said. I just stared at him, not knowing what to say.

"Is there anything I can get for you, books, magazines or anything else? The doctor says you're going to be in here for a little while."

It struck me at that moment that I needed Vitamin E. "I wouldn't mind my Bible, some of my Hot Rod magazines, and the biggest bottle of Vitamin E you can find." Looking around my room I added a request for some clothes as well, but those didn't come until later.

To make a lengthy story shorter, Sgt. McCarthy brought me the biggest bottle of Vitamin E pills he could find. I took three at a time with each meal. My face was covered with Betadine solution to keep the skin moist and any infection at bay, but I had other ideas. I'd heard that Vitamin E would help keep you from having scars. I took a shower to get the Betadine off my face and it hurt like hell. I then broke open several capsules of Vitamin E and covered what was left of my face. I was afraid I would never look normal again. I had blisters all over my face, and a few spots just looked like they melted. I was determined not to follow the prescribed routine every two hours; it was too painful. In my heart I felt the Vitamin E was my only chance to return to a normal life.

After about two hours the nurse came in and shrieked, "What is that on your face?"
"Vitamin E."
"Where's the Betadine solution?"

I pointed to the trash can and she had a cow right there. "Oh no! We'll just see about that."

She stormed out of my room and returned an hour later with the doctor in tow. He silently came to the bedside, took a good long look at my face and asked, "Vitamin E, huh?"

"I'm not going to make you take that off, but the moment we see any sign of infection, it comes off and the Betadine goes back on." I watched the nurse from the corner of my eye as she almost had a stroke. But she bit her tongue and kept her mouth shut. She knew her place was not one of arguing with a doctor.

"That works for me, Doc," I replied through parched lips. I seem to remember he reached into the trash can and took the betadine in hand and sat it on my nightstand. That was Tuesday afternoon, if my memory serves me right. I didn't see the doctor again for a few days, but the nurses were in my room every two hours to check on me. I didn't know if they were coming or going after a while, but there was literally no way a fellow could get much rest with that parade going on.

Friday afternoon the doctor came in and I'd not changed the Vitamin E but once or twice since the previous Tuesday. He looked me over well, then told the nurse to bring a tray of instruments and tools. He began to lift large chunks of scab from my face and lay them on a drape in the tool tray. After about twenty minutes he stopped, looked at me and said, "I think we're going to be able to let you go tomorrow."

They told me six to seven weeks recovery when I came in on Monday morning. Now here I was, going home after only six days. Once they were out of my room, I went to the bathroom mirror and began to thank God for His mercy in my life. I had my face back in seven days, not seven weeks. I had a few small red patches and sore spots, but I had my old face back! I could live as myself again.

I've thought about that several times over the last few years. Had I spent the rest of my life with a disfigured face, I'd have never known that John Wayne might be my grandfather. No one would have asked, "Do you know who you look like?" I thank God that I survived that ordeal without scarring. I have a couple spots on my neck and ears that age has enhanced, but by the healing hand of God I get to live my life as I started.

So, was it my faith in God, or the Vitamin E? I may never have the full answer, but I've learned God uses people, things, and circumstances for our benefit and His Glory. Vitamin E is His work, not ours. With all we have today, we must surely thank Him for His mercy and grace. I'm as undeserving as anyone, but I know without Him we are lost.

The Marine Corps sent me back to Japan after being busted, getting my rank back, and my little experiment with fire. Without going into detail, when a Marine would rather spit in your face than take an order, there's going to be a fight. I lost my restored rank for conduct unbecoming an NCO. A few months later I was called into the CO's office to determine if I was going with my unit to Beirut. Marine Air Base Squadron 36 was headed there and my time in the Marine Corps was drawing short. I told him I wasn't about to re-enlist after being busted twice in two years. At that point, the Marines gave me an early release.

I checked into Camp Pendleton in November 1982 and was given my second honorable discharge. I went home to my wife and children, in Oregon at the time, and went to work for Performance Associates. We sold performance auto parts and did a little work on the side building engines. I also learned front end work at Jerry and Walt's 4 Wheel service. I learned a lot from those old guys, one of which I am now (an old guy). I could write a book on how to become a grumpy old man, but I'll say it in short and easy summation, "Growing old while everything in the world changes around you, but you don't!" It's that simple. That's how you become a grumpy old man. It helps to follow the news. There's nothing good in it.

The following year, in October, someone blew up the Marine barracks in Beirut and two hundred Marines lost their lives. One of them could have been me. To this day I don't know if my squadron was still there. Terrorists have been attacking the US for years, and we never responded in any meaningful way until 9/11. Now they live amongst us and we're going to catch hell for it. People who hate us are getting elected and appointed to powerful government offices...well, I'd better stop there.

A person doesn't change overnight, but change was certainly upon me. Life has not been easy for me, but I wouldn't change anything. It's been an adventure, a real roller coaster ride, but trouble has taught me a lot that nothing else could. I'm proud of my Marine Corps heritage because when I look around at many folks my age and younger, it seems at this writing, I'm pretty healthy at sixty-four and 295 pounds.

It's odd to me that I can still remember our phone number from the fourth grade, as well as my Aunt Wilma's number across the street. But I can't remember where I left my glasses five minutes ago. I'll be sixty-five in 2023 and my eyes were perfect until I took a job welding trains a few years ago. But if I'm supposed to lose my sight I know where the typing keys are on the keyboard. I can still say what I think with my hands. I took typing in the tenth grade at Osage High School in Independence. I'd spent the previous fall and winter in Poplar Bluff doing the same. I can type with ease, though it took a while to retrain my hands to a modern computer keyboard. Writing novels like "Blood Once Spilled", "Peace in the Valley", and "Showdown at Scatter Creek" made for good practice.

CHAPTER 5
A DESTINY TAKES HOLD

While driving home from my father's funeral, which my grandmother attended, my wife declared out of the blue, "If you're going to start publishing all those westerns you've been writing, you might want to look like a cowboy!"

Those honest words changed my life, my future, forever. I didn't realize the power held within her words, or how they would change my life in so many ways. Neither did she. They marked the reawakening of my heritage mystery and the beginning of my quest for knowledge concerning the cover-up of my father's birth. It might be said, "You can't just start dressing differently and change your life." As The Duke would have said, "The Hell you can't!" Change the way you dress and see what happens.

This then was my new beginning. At six-feet-four and the age of fifty-one I had no idea how that one statement would affect the rest of my life. I bought my first western hat, leather jacket, a vest, boots, and other essentials within a few short weeks. It was the first time in almost fifty years I looked like a cowboy since I was three-years old wearing a set of cap pistols. What I didn't expect was the faint image of John Wayne coming forth from the mirror. It was more than that, I'm built like The Duke; tall and lanky which affects the way I walk, with some people seeing me said, "Just like The Duke." I can't help it, there's no practice needed unless you call walking my dog practice. It's just natural for me. So are my movements and mannerisms. There's not a thing I can do about it. Sometimes I lose my voice, but when I have all of it, I sound like The Duke as well. So, what happened eighty-eight years ago? Genes don't get handed down by kissing.

What I don't want missed is at this point our grandmother was still very much alive. She was at my father's funeral and still didn't offer anything in the way of an answer. I personally thought she owed us one, but she did not come forth. What happened in the spring of 1934 was her business. I tried to bring it up a few months later, when I stopped by to visit her, but as always, it was a taboo subject.

In 2009, when we buried our father, Granny was ninety-one years old. I had never seen her as a young person, she was Granny my entire life.

The Author's Paternal Grandmother (R), with his dad as a child by the back wheel of the truck @1940

The first time I laid eyes on her she was a gray-haired grandma wearing glasses. That's what I saw whenever my eyes focused upon her. So, how in the world would someone like John Wayne have any interest in my grandmother? She wasn't always a grandmother, nor a mother. At the time she met my dad's real father (Memorial Day Weekend 1934) she was drop dead gorgeous. That's what I didn't understand. My own mind would not calculate that until I saw an actual picture of her at nineteen. The family isn't exactly going to hand me that picture at this point, because it helps prove what happened. Once upon a time, grandmothers were very pretty young girls. Having nine children changes all that.

    The photo in question was shown to me by my aunt, but I've not seen it since. I may never.

CHAPTER 6
HOLD EVERYTHING, JOE JITSU

After leaving Granny's house, I began my search and went to the newspaper in Hickman, Kentucky where they directed me to the library on the hill. I discovered there was certainly a party in Hickman on Memorial Day 1934. It was a graduation celebration by Doctor John C. Morrison for his daughter. Martha had recently graduated from Duke University Law School. Were Martha and John cousins? Fans might also recognize that Memorial Day (May 26, 1934) is John Wayne's birthday. The Duke would have been twenty-six years old that weekend. A few old timers recall he had been in town once or twice, but that was all they could remember. I wondered if The Duke ever crashed a party or started one of his own?

I learned as a young Marine that you can have too much to drink and not remember how you got somewhere. That one experience stopped me from drinking. Perhaps that's what happened with my grandmother? She certainly wouldn't have been used to drinking, just as I wasn't when I joined the Marines. She could have been taken with the handsome John, and he with her, considering she was prettier than all of John Wayne's wives put together! Nine months later, in late February nineteen thirty-five, she was giving birth to my father. I'm no mathematician, but I can count to nine months. Coincidence? So why all the secrecy? Why not just tell us boys who our grandfather is? Well, John Wayne was married to his first wife Josephine at the time, and she was at home pregnant with Michael. Not a good scenario for the studios, John Wayne, or Josephine, for that matter.

Is it any wonder The Duke's first marriage didn't last? We all know John was away from home and traveled a lot. He even managed to ride in parades in Dallas, Texas, Washington, and many other places around the country. The Rose Bowl Parade, Macy's

Thanksgiving Day Parade; the list is endless. John Wayne was a well-traveled man, and most times his wife was at home pregnant or with the children attending school.

Some of his known affairs are not even questioned, such as Marlene Dietrich and Pat Stacy. My question is when did his philandering really begin? I suppose we may never know the true answer, but I do believe one of them happened with Lela Pearl Clemens in Hickman, Kentucky in the spring of 1934. It was *his* birthday, and there was a celebration on top of the hill at Dr. Morrison's home. Dr. Morrison, the 32nd degree Mason and eventually the man who would deliver all of Granny's children. From the evidence I have seen so far, I do believe he delivered all nine of them, including my father.

CHAPTER 7
MY LIFE BEGINS

Once I left home and became Terry Wayne Hammock, United States Marine, I never believed the unanswered question concerning our true heritage would ever again come into play. Even when I reached my fifties it had become the farthest thought from my mind. However, since the family was not going to provide answers, I wasn't going to let them ruin what life I did have.

I loved reading good westerns and had plans to make my own way as the next Louis L'Amour. I didn't need to know where I came from to be myself, to chase my dreams. I knew who I was, I really did, right up to the moment I took my first step into a new chapter in my life and landed face first on the ground! If you were ever a Marine, you know what I'm talking about. Bends and thrusts, pushups, side-straddle hops, and more…for three months you live face down in the dirt. When you again become an upright animal, you find there's some meat on your bones. I went from 170 pounds to 215 in just three months. My lieutenant called me "Horse" because I carried everything he handed me. I was a good Marine, one of the best, I felt, but trouble has a nasty way of determining for a man what he does during the day.

Everyone has those times when they're ready to take on the world and they get knocked down, HARD. You get back up, only to be slammed face first into the tarmac of life once again. After getting trampled a few times one might ask himself, "What the hell? Why is this happening to me? Nothing has gone as planned!" You find yourself way behind, so you take off again, this time with a bit more caution, only to get blindsided by someone you trusted, a family member or close friend maybe. Such things create trust issues for a young person. Your judgment becomes tainted because you no longer trust anyone.

One thing I learned from all the turmoil: your dreams must exceed your fears. Your dreams must remain constant, and you cannot let fear get in your way. It becomes tougher to hold onto your dreams once you've been beaten down by life from the starting gate. Even from last place, if you hang on to hope, you can hang on to your dreams. The Rolling Stones wrote in the nineteen-sixties, "Lose your dreams and you will lose your mind." Those words ring in my head every day. Hang onto your dreams, if you never have anything else, hang onto them.

A young man's dreams must exceed his fears.
~John T. Wayne

CHAPTER 8
LIFE DOESN'T LET UP

When I lost my daughter Kimberly to cancer in the winter of 1985, I'd just about had enough. At that point I didn't care much for anyone or anything. I was quite literally a fish out of water and losing my mind at the age of twenty-six. It's ironic that The Duke met my grandmother in Hickman, Kentucky at the age of twenty-six, making movies (and babies!). Most of my friends owned homes and had families by twenty-six, while I was no longer sure about anything. For the next few years, I moped around feeling sorry for myself. If someone wanted to get into my face or start an argument at work, I just picked up my things and walked off the job. Life and my temper were too short to properly deal with a bully who didn't recognize what I was going through. Besides, after knocking one man out cold with one punch I was afraid that I might kill the next one unintentionally.

I didn't seek psychiatric help. That was not our family way; not then, not now. I handled things my own way. I turned to the one thing I still love: classic automobiles. They never betray me, and I understand them. They don't talk back, they obey commands well, and they will never tell lies about you behind your back! Having owned many, I gained a deep appreciation for classic lines found on an old car or truck. I always find a challenge in making them better than ever, and it keeps my mind off unpleasant things, like burying my children. That's how I made it through until I met my wife, Donna. She lets me lean on her and she understands me, though there were times I didn't realize it. She's my biggest cheerleader. In 2015 she helped me buy our 1960 Thunderbird, now known as the "True Grit Thunderbird", because she knew an old car was about the only thing that made sense to me.

Another change I made after losing my daughter to cancer was that I began to write in earnest. I figured if I was ever going to make it, I had to figure out who I was all over again. Her death scrambled my brain, as if the dyslexia I suffered all through my school years wasn't enough. I began to write my thoughts and feelings down on paper, sorting out life's truths from fiction and I began to heal. Writing and the grace of God got me through some tough times, often crying over my loss. Sometimes I still do, like when it's Kimberly's birthday and I can't do anything for her. The only way I could heal was to write, separating truth from fiction, even though my family story looked more like fiction than fact. I still didn't know anything beyond my father and his mother. I can't have a conversation about it, the whole thing only upsets family to this day. It leaves a young man bewildered. Losing my daughter didn't even rattle the family cage concerning my dead-end heritage. But it doesn't matter, because all things happen in God's time, not ours.

After six months of writing everything that came to mind, I had a strange revelation: "If I'm going to write this much, maybe I should just write a novel." I learned, while stationed in Japan, that I liked Louis L'Amour westerns. He wrote over 120 books, mostly westerns but in other genres as well. More than thirty of them were made into western movies such as "Hondo" (starring John Wayne), "How the West Was Won", and "Shadow Riders". So, with not much thought about what my story would be, I began "Life of a Dead Man." Today that book is "The Treasure del Diablo." I saved the original title for Part II.

To be honest, I'm still healing almost forty years later. I've heard that you never heal. I write to remember who I am, to honor the life of my daughter, and to offer insight into life that others may not have experienced. The things I've learned in my lifetime are unique because they came about from circumstances I had little to do with. I live each day to the fullest knowing that God Almighty is in charge, not me. I'm still learning how to react when bad things happen because I don't know what is coming down the track next. Whatever it may be, I'm thankful for every full day I get.

There have been times I have paused, looked to Heaven and spoken directly to God. I've asked, "Are you really going to let this happen?" When we lost our son Ryan Richard in 2007, I was so angry I was spitting bullets and cursing God. I finally realized that God had nothing to do with Ryan's death, someone else was responsible. When I married Donna, she came with three sons from a previous marriage: John Thomas, Ryan Richard, and Beau Vincent Davis. I loved and raised them as my own.

Writing has helped me recover from losing Kimberly and Ryan Richard. I concluded that suicide is the most selfish form of behavior on this planet. The victim has no thought of others or doesn't care about their pain and grief, only their own. You see, each person, tree, animal, and flower on earth was put here for a reason. We are all here to help each other, not hurt one another. Just as the bee needs the flower and the flower needs the bee, they both need the rain and the sun to survive. "Sincere need" means there are no skin colors, ethnic roots, or economic differences. A person contemplating suicide is unable to get out of their own selfishness to see the love and beauty surrounding them. For whatever reason, they believe life will never be better. All they see is a horrible situation with no end, and they don't believe they can do anything about it.

I learned the hard way, through tough lessons in this life, that I need to live what I believe. I didn't come by my convictions lightly. I learned when you're born you don't get to pick your family, and you certainly don't get to pick the circumstances you were born into. When you think about it, someone else made a lot of decisions for you long before you were given life.

When looking at a photo of Rooster Cogburn, I realized decisions made long ago brought me to have the same front teeth, the same lazy eye, the same ears, the same facial features.

The Author dressed as "Rooster Cogburn".

Hoot Gibson was a famous cowboy who ran with John Wayne, Roy Rogers, Tom Mix, Rex Allen, and others. They were all admired movie stars from the 1930s and beyond. All those men worked hard and played hard, with maybe the exception of Roy, who was a devoted family man.

The Author at the Tom Mix Museum, Dewey, Oklahoma

The same was said of John Wayne, though by all accounts, he loved the attention of the ladies, especially when he was away from home. He was married three times, and according to all known accounts, he had seven children. Yet, I contest those accounts as I lay claim to my true "American Heritage". You must admit, there was no bigger flag waving, America-loving cowboy than The Duke himself. But how many names can be used to name the children in one family? I refer to my father's half-brothers and sisters who are coincidentally named for The Duke and his children.

I believe that's how God works. When men do something to cover the truth, God allows certain clues to remain so the truth can be found. The truth can be hidden, but like a bubble in the ocean, it will eventually come to the surface. I think we can agree that God understands time better than we do. His time is without limit, while ours is not, at least not yet.

What I offer is the truth to the best of my knowledge. There are so many lies being perpetrated in our world today, the last thing I want to do is add to the problem. I can't tell a bunch of lies under the eyes of God and live with myself. Checking and rechecking the things I'm telling you became a strict requirement. I plan to be here a long time after this book is released, and the last thing I want to do is publish a bunch of lies.

CHAPTER 9
NEW TREE BRANCHES

A few years ago, I was invited to sign books at the annual Civil War reunion at the Columbus Belmont State Park in Kentucky. It was there I was given the following story:

In 1971 Lyle Edwards was with the San Diego Police Department. He received a call of a Domestic Disturbance at around two in the morning at a local all-night diner. When Officer Edwards entered the establishment there was a tall man standing with his back to the door. He walked up to the man, spun him around and nearly fainted. It was John Wayne. Gathering himself, he said, "Mr. Wayne, it's time to go home. Why don't you let me give you a ride?"

Officer Edwards gave him that ride and the two of them became good friends. It never hurts to have a friend in the Police Department when you have a habit of overstaying your welcome. He took Mr. Wayne to the marina where his private boat was docked and helped him aboard. A third divorce for Wayne was looming and he wanted to drink it off his mind...

There have been several stories like this that people have relayed to me about the old Duke, from firsthand encounters or second parties who were there at the time. But that's a book of a different kind that tells a side of John Wayne that people are not familiar with. I'm still collecting those stories and I'll share them at some time in the future so people will get to know The Duke even better. I get these stories handed to me while I am out signing my own books.

As the number of stories began to grow, I should have known something was amiss. After my father died and my wife suggested I start to dress the part of an author of westerns, people began to tell me how much I looked like John Wayne, but no one in my life ever told me that I could be related to The Duke in any way. In fact, my father's family went out of their way to make certain I never had any idea who my grandfather really was.

As a child I learned of the Bible stories of Cain killing his brother, Able, and of Joseph's nine brothers selling him into slavery for twenty pieces of silver while telling their father he was eaten by an evil beast. But those are ancient stories in far-away lands. Modern men didn't do things like that anymore. Boy, was I wrong!

I never considered facts such as having an Uncle John, Uncle Wayne, Aunt Pat, Aunt Mary Ann, and Uncle Robert, all of which had John Wayne family names. I still didn't see any possible connection even though my father looked just like the actor. I never gave it a thought until I began to look so much like my father and the actor myself. I, Terry Wayne Hammock, a man who didn't want to be anything like my father, slowly morphed into exactly that. Even though my dad was crippled, he was the spitting image. I still didn't get it because I still didn't see what everyone else saw in me.

Finally, at age fifty-two, it seemed I couldn't go anywhere without someone saying something about my resemblance to John Wayne. I waited twenty plus years to publish my first book, and as my westerns were coming out in sequence, I was doing book signings around the country. People told me things I simply could no longer ignore or deny, things like, "Good Lord, you stand just like The Duke", "You're built like The Duke", "You sound just like The Duke"…!

The possibility that my dad's existence was swept under the Hollywood rug like unwanted dirt in 1935 was starting to bother me. Most children born with Spina-Bifida at that time didn't survive for very long. But dad had an ace up his sleeve. His grandmother Clements was also born with Spina-Bifida and had survived. It was she who took him in as one of her own and raised him with the name Billy Gene Clements until he could no longer be ignored. Cloaked in complete secrecy my father never had any idea of the events that led to his birth. He was too busy trying to grow up and get around. I believe, if he had known of his true origins, he would have been in California claiming his heritage and his share of John Wayne Enterprises. But Granny never explained to him his birthright. She never gave him a truthful account of who his real father was. Had she told dad, she would have also had to tell the other eight children she had, so they were kept in the dark as well. It's my belief she didn't want to wreck the family narrative created when my father was born. She was only sixteen when she became pregnant, so she did what she was told. In the last few years many of the hidden pieces of that puzzle have come to light. Many of the answers walked right up to my table while I was signing books in different places around the country.

I think Granny, at some point, gave in and told the other children, the ones she had to live with every day, that my dad's father was Victor Hammock, but only out of frustration. She never said a word to us boys. I think it was because she knew he wasn't my dad's father. She just dealt with matters the best she could without blowing the lid off and breaking whatever pact she might have made with The Duke. She offered them what I call "Old Reliable," the name on dad's birth certificate. I mean really, who would question that?

I'll bet not many of you knew or understood who you were going to be from an early age, regardless of your roots. That's the secret of John Wayne's American creed, which is why he was so special. He had a vision, and everything he did, after a few scrapes with uncharted destiny, was focused on that vision. It was because of that vision that he became an American legend. I have a vision, too. I would love for my western novels to be revered like westerns my grandfather did for the movie business. Big boots to fill, but we shall see.

When a man sees his destiny, he should stay the course. But sometimes distractions come along and push us into uncharted waters. They could be an enemy we didn't expect, an accident, or some other force or event which does not help our cause or shakes the foundation we were building upon. Sometimes just meeting someone and letting things get out of hand can do it, such as what happened with my grandmother and The Duke in 1934.

I want folks to consider that my father could actually be The Duke's son, and I want them to know the truth. Had my father been born to one of The Duke's three wives the entire world would know that I'm John Wayne's grandson. But that was not the case, and the tangled web of lies and cover-ups, woven to hide my fathers' birth, follows within these pages.

I never heard my grandfather's name mentioned until I attended my Uncle Russell's funeral when I was about fifty years old. Even then, the name I was given wasn't my grandfather at all. It was just the old family lie to keep this bloodhound off the trail, but I finally had something to investigate. At the funeral, my aunt told me she had a letter from Granny for us three boys, but she promised Granny she wouldn't give it to us until Granny was gone; suddenly I had a glimmer of hope. She also told me my grandfather was buried "on yon hill", at the same cemetery where we were putting Uncle Russell to rest. She said his name was Victor Hammock. *Viola! I had a name!* Mind you, I was fifty-one years old, but I had a name, only to find out, this, too, was a dead end. I had not seen my fathers' birth certificate yet, but what I learned didn't add up.

The obituary for Victor Hammock says Victor had two sons: William (Bill) and Larry. Bill died in a car wreck in nineteen-seventy-nine, and Larry died the same year as my father, two-thousand-nine. So, who then was Billy Gene Hammock/Clements? He would be a third son, only there was no third son. And who would call or name two sons Bill?

It should be noted here that I have never met any of the people listed here or their descendants. If Victor Hammock was my father's real father, wouldn't we know them as family? We lived in Union City, Tennessee for two years in 1968 and 1969, less than fifteen miles from all these folks, and we never visited a single one? The only family we had in Tennessee and Kentucky was the Gordon family of father's half-brothers and sisters. That's it. So, who are the Hammocks? Why don't any of them show up in my DNA test, like the Gordons and some of the Morrisons? Why are so many of the Morrisons' records marked as private? There's a lot of questions I do not have answers to, but if you will allow me the time, I do have more pieces of the puzzle to complete a pretty good picture.

I had the chance in 2016, while digging into this oddity, to speak with a lady named Shockey Jones, who was Victor Hammock's sister-in-law. Not only was she certain that Victor only had the two boys, but she had also been friends with my grandmother. They rode to work together, and Shockey never heard of my father. For even more strangeness, Shockey and my father were both born in Hickman, Kentucky in the same year. Wouldn't she remember a crippled little boy she went to school with? I sure would. I might forget the name, but I wouldn't forget a crippled classmate. But here again, Shockey Jones only knew one Bill Hammock, her nephew, but never heard of a second one! What is going on in Hickman, Kentucky?

If it was okay for Granny's family to disclose the information after Uncle Russell's funeral, why couldn't we have that information while we were growing up? Why was it so important to keep such a secret until it no longer mattered? Well, you can't dig up the dead and ask them about it, that's why. The family knew the chances of one of us finding the truth about our heritage by then would be next to impossible. Those who covered up my father's birth, and the family who agreed to hide the truth from him, underestimated the power of Almighty God to reveal the truth. Some folks consider faith in God and His power to be a weakness. I'll take that weakness any time, and I'll take God's planning over mine any day of the week. Life is fraught with chance and circumstance that only God can account for.

AN AMERICAN HERITAGE

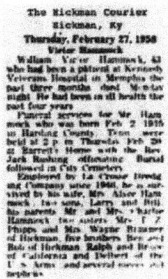

Photo added by .A

William Victor Hammock

BIRTH 2 Feb 1915
Hardin County, Tennessee, USA

DEATH 17 Feb 1958 (aged 43)
Memphis, Shelby County, Tennessee, USA

BURIAL Hickman City Cemetery
Hickman, Fulton County, Kentucky, USA

MEMORIAL ID 161353576 ·

Family Members

Parents

Charles Robert Hammock
1880–1960

Mary Alice *Jones* Hammock
1889–1964

Spouse

Alyce M *Jones* Hammock
1923–2002 (m. (marriage) 1941)

Siblings

Aubrey Ralph Hammock
1903–1971

Arthur Benton Hammock
1905–1992

James Wynegar Hammock
1907–1953

Robert L Hammock
1909–1979

Estelle *Hammock* Phipps
1913 – unknown

Mary Ruth Hammock
1917–1918

Children

Robert Lee Hammock
1946–1947

Victor Hammock who is NOT the Author's grandfather!

My brothers and I knew something had happened, and we always had hope of getting a clue. We had no deadline and we all just let it ride for years figuring we would never know. For fifty years we were in the dark about our heritage, until my dad passed away in 2009.

Growing up I was very familiar with the name John Wayne. He was a great American, cowboy actor, and hero. Many times, I went to the theater to watch him on the big screen. This compounds the problem of finding the truth because you can't besmirch the name of a popular American hero and get away with it. The American public will defend their heroes and forgive any indiscretions, me included. Like my grandmother, I believe he was in way over his head and did what he was told to save his Hollywood career. My grandmother was only seventeen when my father was born on February 21, 1935, nine months after they met on that Memorial Day in May 1934. The Duke's wife, Josephine, was at home and pregnant with their son Michael at the time my father was conceived. Michael was born November 23, 1934, my father February 21, 1935, only three months apart. Were they half-brothers? By strange coincidence, my wife Donna and I have celebrated our anniversary on *November 23rd* every year since 1990.

It is not my place to judge. It is also not my intention to tarnish the name of John Wayne, in any way, but to bring to light that he could likely have *at least eight* children. I have been contacted by other families over the ten years while I've been trying to assemble the pieces of my own life puzzle.

CHAPTER 10
A TRUE AMERICAN

    I can only testify for my father who lived his entire life and died without knowing his father was possibly John Wayne. I will not reveal any others out of respect for their right to privacy. Rather, my intention is to reveal the truth. A branch of the Wayne family was possibly broken from the family tree under the weight of a Hollywood image, landed under a veil of secrecy and deception for eighty-eight years, while everyone learned to be fine with it. It was through the power of God we were able to find the truth behind our father's birth. Billy Gene Hammock knew his Heavenly Father well. Now he knows of his true American Heritage.

    My father was known as Billy Gene Hammock. However, as a young boy he was raised as Billy Gene Clements. He knew who his mother was, but not his father. It was hard enough living life as a cripple and those added family lies hurt him deeply. The number of years the family carried on the deception may be in question, but I believe the lie itself was never in doubt. The family probably felt they had no choice but to lie to him, or so they believed. It seems the lie began with my great-grandparents, but for some reason our father was known as Billy Gene Clements in his early years. He had no reason to believe anything different.

Billy Gene Clements, the Author's father at age 11

I mention my great grandparents, John Thomas and Rose Clements, because it's with them the lie began. They never wavered.

In the late summer of 2011, I placed a call to the National Enquirer because my life was beginning to spin out of control. The fellow I spoke with had a foreign accent and informed me that "it takes more than looking like someone to be their grandson." He laughed and hung up. He was right, of course, but he didn't stay on the phone long enough to hear the gist of my story or the rest of my evidence, or as the late great radio newsman Paul Harvey said on his daily afternoon show, "The Rest of the Story". At the time, I was hoping they would help me with some discovery and research, but all I got was a dismissive laugh and a dial tone.

Imagine, having grown up thinking your last name was one thing when it was actually something else. That sort of thing could drive a lot of people crazy, but not my father. Dad had something built in that wouldn't let family or anyone else get in his way. When he put his foot down, you knew you'd crossed a line. Our father was stern and corrected us with a belt more than once. Though he was crippled, or handicapped as we say today, he was all man.

A father's love without correction is no love at all!
~John T. Wayne

We boys never dreamed that our father didn't have any idea, but we sure knew it was a sore subject with him, and none of our business. He had a short temper on the grandpa subject, probably because it left a hole in his heart. When the lie started, he was living as the youngest son of John Thomas and Rose Clements. His big sister got married in 1940 and became Lela Pearl Gordon. Billy Gene only knew his birth mother as his big sister, though he would learn much later that was not correct. The name Hammock confuses things even more.

I have this nagging question in my mind: he spent his school years as a Clements, being told his mother was his sister. Was this so the Hammock family would not discover he was named for them? It's a reasonable question. Hickman, Kentucky isn't that big of a town. Why let him think his last name was Clements all those years? He and Shockey Jones were of the same age, why didn't she know of him? I think it was because she knew him as Billy Gene Clements, not the other Bill Hammock.

As Dad became a teenager, what he learned, or surmised about his family, didn't please him. Not upset with his mother so much, but with his grandparents who pretended to be his mom and dad. When he learned that everyone in his immediate family had been lying to him, he packed up and left. I don't believe his seventeen-year-old mother cooked up the idea of playing the part of his sister until such time as the truth could no longer be hidden. No, the lie and deception involved the entire Clements family, and continues to this day. They still maintain much of the lie, though the name has been changed over the years to Gordon because of marriage. Why? I believe it's because they'd have to also accept that they were also lied to. They cannot believe to this day their own mother would lie to them! The census shows there is no mention yet of the name Hammock. Dad believed he was a "Clements" and that was told to the census takers in nineteen forty.

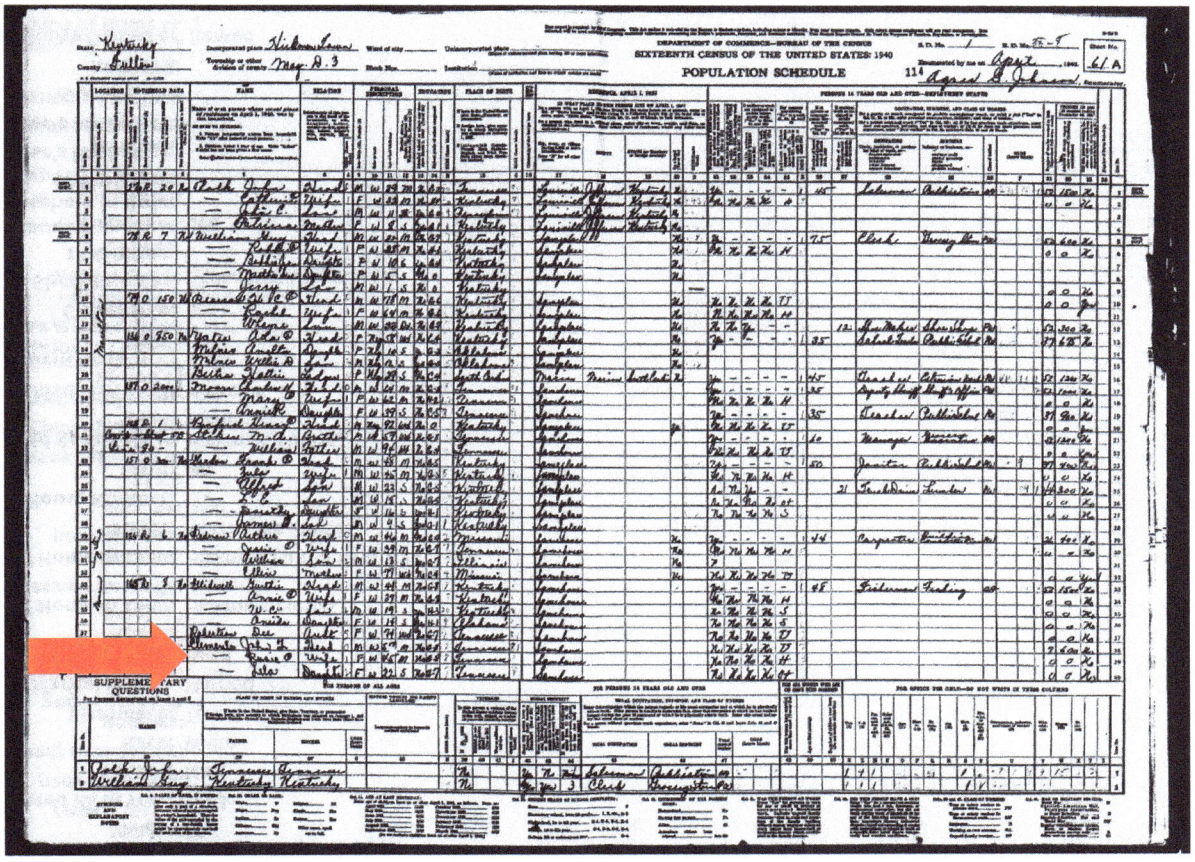

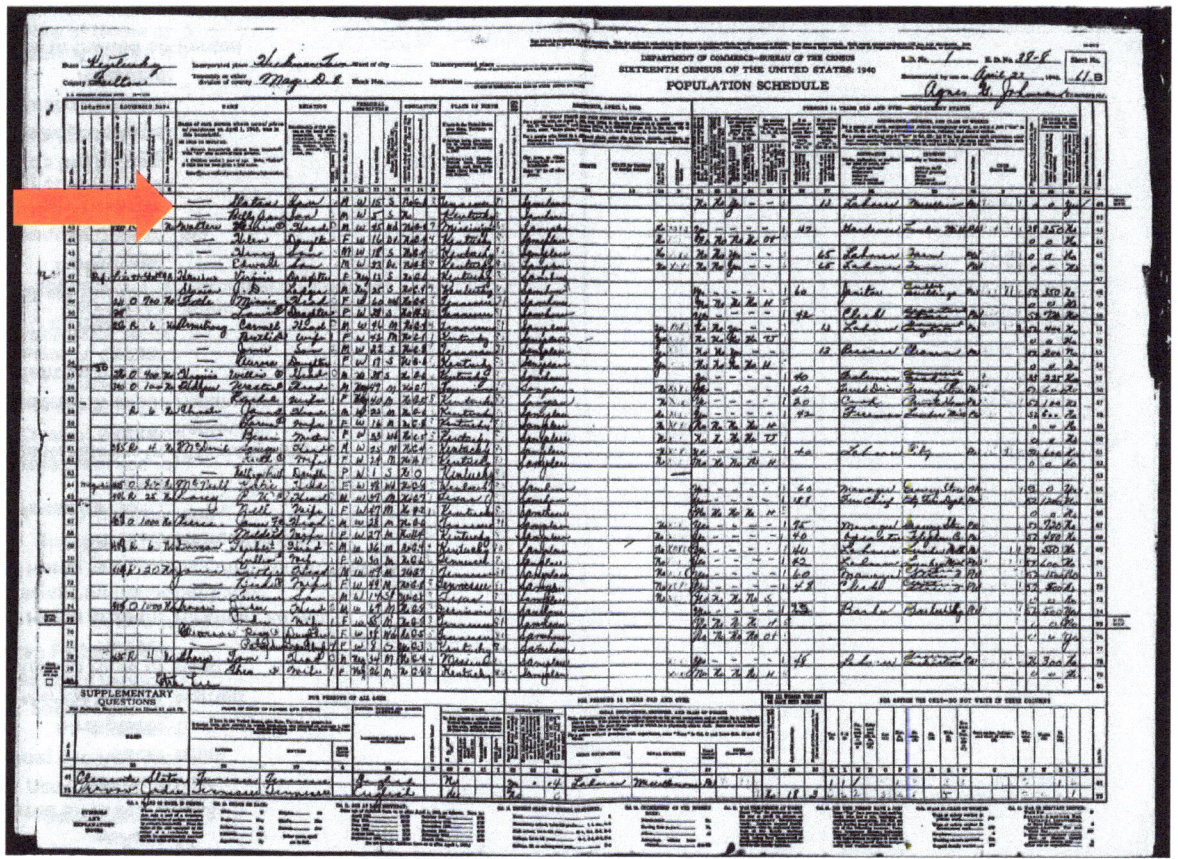

The 1940 Census reinforces that Billy Gene was a Clements.

My dad's half-brothers and sisters are not included because they weren't born yet. But I don't believe they knew the truth, either. They may have suspected there were some discrepancies in the family history, but it was understood early on that "we don't talk about that". The blanket denial and avoidance of the issue, from 1935 by my great grandparents on down, was impenetrable until one does the math.

Math done correctly will always expose a lie.

~John T. Wayne

Now, people make mistakes and do things they shouldn't. If my father's existence was the result of ordinary people giving in to temptation, it wouldn't be something to be proud of, but certainly not the subject of Top-Secret level of secrecy, deception, falsehoods and lies that this mystery involves. Therefore, it must have involved someone famous or important. In this case Victor Hammock does not qualify, but John Wayne does. My point is quite simple: if it was some average Joe in the next town, why not just give it up? No, it had to be somebody, and was John Wayne that somebody? We have evidence that he had the reputation, the opportunity, the means, the connections, and the altered legal documentation backed by firsthand stories from folks who knew the truth.

Often in my life I suffered under the idea that I was cursed, that I had upon me one of those generational curses which the Bible alludes to. To wit: "When cursed by both God and the Devil, God is the only one who is remotely interested in lifting the curse."

Not a thing in the names Billy Gene Clements or Billy Gene Hammock indicates he was the son of John Wayne. Yet, after ten years of searching, with complete strangers providing tidbits of information, it is possible to conclude that the lies began with my father's birth, and consequently his birth certificate. There are few photos of my dad because of his handicap. There are five generations of the same genes creating the same look, features and manner within a family which suggests there must be a common link because fabricating a gene is something that man cannot do.

I don't think or believe that Marion Morrison didn't know or forgot about our father. He didn't contact him, but I don't believe he wanted things that way. He just didn't know what The Duke should do under the circumstances. Ironically, he took a roll in the movie "Shepherd of the Hills" where he played the part of a young man whose family lied to him about his real father. Personally, it's my opinion that he took the part to at least get a feeling for what my dad felt. I also feel The Duke had help from Hollywood, the Masons, and the Catholic Church to keep his likely second son, Billy Gene Hammock, from ever becoming known.

AN AMERICAN HERITAGE

Registrar of Vital Statistics
Certified Copy

I received a copy of Dad's Birth Certificate while I was writing "Showdown at Scatter Creek". It looked as I expected but I was against a writing deadline, so it languished on my writing desk for some time. About six months passed when a passing glance at it got my attention: *ALL OF THE LEGAL SIGNATURES WERE IN THE SAME HANDWRITING!* I had already accepted that my father was listed as legitimate at birth but assumed that was probably an error. As I began to realize something wasn't right, I looked at the document in greater detail. There was no state stamp or seal, and the names of mother and father were not typed in. Their signatures were in the same handwriting as the others. Can you do that? I think it's considered forgery to sign someone else's name. Finally, I was told by the family that Doctor Morrison delivered all my grandmother's children. But my dad's altered Birth Certificate was signed by Doctor Baker!

"The truth will come to the surface."

~John T. Wayne

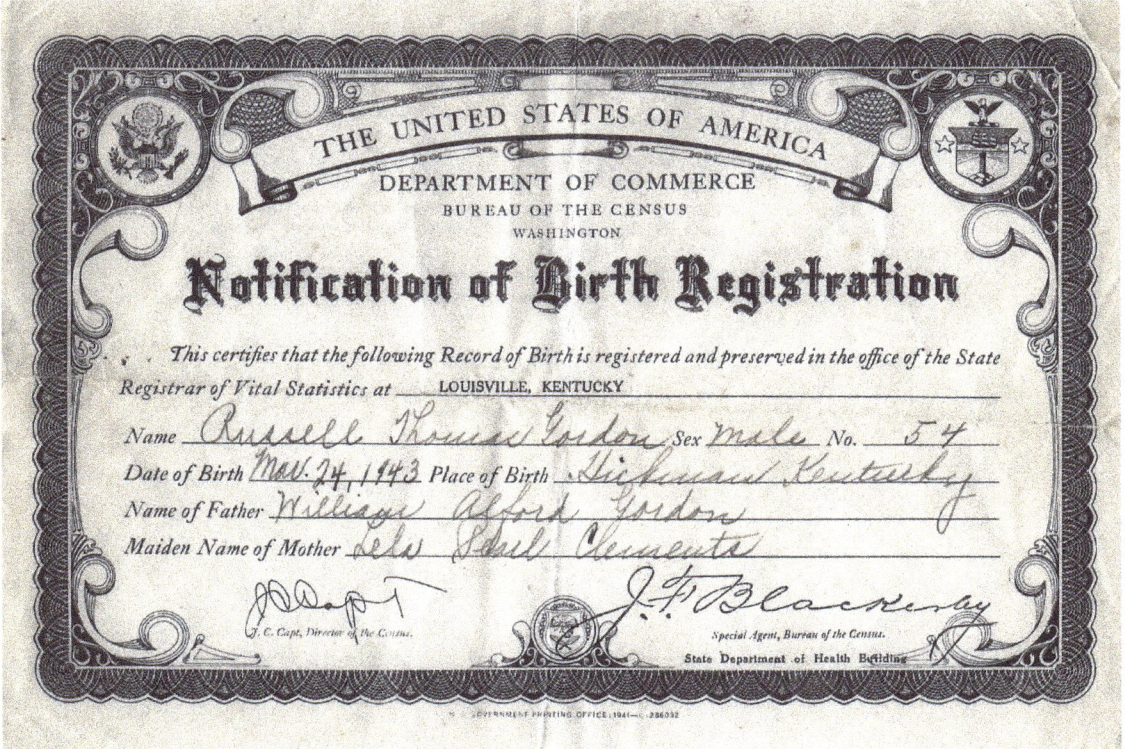

When comparing the Statement of Birth for my Uncle Russell, yet another child delivered by Doctor John C. Morrison, the handwriting is smooth and flowing and the same as what is on my father's birth certificate. It has come to light that this is not Dr. Morrison's handwriting, but perhaps his nurse or office clerk. So, who worked for Dr. Morrison but signed the name of Dr. Baker on my father's birth certificate? That's very odd! The only mention I have found of Dr. Baker in Hickman, Kentucky was 1901-1916. My grandmother was born in *1917*! No, I don't think Dr. Baker was the attending physician, because how many doctors employ the same clerk? We also know that Dr. Baker would have been approximately ninety-three when dad was born, so what is going on here? Did Dr. Baker live that long? If so, was he still delivering babies? See the problem?

At the time I was discovering all of this, I was sitting at my desk when the phone rang. It was a good friend named Sylvia Evans, who was a genealogy specialist for Poinsett County, Arkansas. She also had a copy of my dad's birth certificate, and she didn't believe it, either. She was taking valuable time to see if there was anything else out there to find.

"John, are you sitting down?"

"Of course, I'm at my desk finishing up 'Scatter Creek'. What's up?"

"John, your father has two birth certificates! John? Hello, John?"

After some silence, I finally answered, "I'm here."

I spoke with Sylvia at length, and she had found the sealed documents. The clerk from the bureau of Vital Statistics had told her, "We can't give you these! Do you know who this is?" and she hung up the phone. "I haven't been able to get her back. I know they have had it sealed up for all these years."

Generally, records that are public but sealed are so because someone convinced a judge to hide them. After this many years it's obvious we are being stonewalled. I don't have the money to hire a lawyer to petition a court to unseal records which may provide an answer to my dad's true ancestry. My hope is that his book will help me shake the true document loose from the grip of the State of Kentucky.

As my father was growing up in and out of the hospital while attending school, he was required to provide a Birth Certificate. The family had to begrudgingly hand him the only one they had. Since he was always known as Billy Gene Clements it was no doubt a shock to learn his name was Hammock. Could it be that the name Victor Hammock was used just to complete the Birth Certificate, not his correct name of Morrison or Wayne? Why not? Victor didn't sign it, and Granny didn't sign it because someone signed it for them both. It also seems there is no record that Doctor Baker continued working after Morrison arrived in 1921. Added to the apparent forgery, my father's birth certificate states he was legitimate at birth to father William Victor Hammock and mother Lela Pearl Clements. They were never married. How is that considered legitimate?

I concede that Victor Hammock of Hickman, Kentucky did exist. He had a son they called Bill, but that son died in a car wreck in 1979. Clearly it was not my father in that accident because he lived another thirty years. There was another son named Larry and one who died at one year old. There is no other record of my father in the Hammock family of Hickman, Kentucky. So, where did dad come from?

I believe my father went to see Victor in Hickman. I think he discovered he was not Victor's son, hence his silence on the issue. By then Victor was suffering from cancer. Our father thought his name was Clements. His poorly forged Birth Certificate says his name was Hammock, but even that turned out to be a lie. I've been digging for a long time, and it sure seems unlikely Doctor Baker of Hickman, Kentucky delivered any of Granny's children. Baker would have been ninety-three for dad, ninety-eight for Uncle Wayne, over one hundred years old for Aunt Pat, Mary Ann and Uncle Bobby. The family has stated that Doctor John C. Morrison delivered them. It means there is no trace of a family prior to our father, one Billy Gene Hammock. Our father was a young man with no answers. With no clear answer, only lies to speak of, he probably felt silence was the best thing.

Circumstances being food for question, we know Dr. Morrison and Walter Ruby, both from Kentucky, and Marion Morrison (John Wayne) were all 32nd degree Masons. (*A 32nd degree mason is a Freemason who has been recognized for his knowledge of Freemasonry and for his service to the community. A 32nd degree mason has gone through extensive training in Freemasonry and has demonstrated his dedication to the organization. He has also shown his commitment to helping others by performing various service projects.* ~ https://www.meaningfulspaces.com/what-is-a-32-mason/.)

A party was held on Memorial Day weekend in 1934 at Dr. Morrison's home which overlooked the Mississippi River. Nine months later, almost to the day, my father was born to a seventeen-year-old young lady from Hickman who was at that party. The remainder of her eight children were delivered by Dr. Morrison. Though there is no lineage to support it, Dad was supposed to be part of the Hammock family. Yet they made no effort to include him, or even speak with him, even though he lived right there!

So where is the truth? I contend it begins with a sealed document guarded by the Bureau of Vital Statistics in Frankfort. In our case the truth was so well hidden it has outlived two generations, and nearly a third, and no one will tell us why. They're all gone by now.

As I said earlier, people, stories and evidence just appear without warning. One of my most interesting exchanges came in 2013 as I was visiting the John Wayne Birthplace Museum in Winterset, Iowa. Parking my wife's Cadillac on the street after making the 600-mile drive, I made my way to the old house where a line of people gathered outside along the white picket fence. I asked one of the folks in line what was going on and a woman spoke up with the answer.

"Maureen O'Hara is inside. We're waiting to see her."

Just then the side door opened, and Ms. O'Hara emerged in a wheelchair pushed by her grandson. Now, I'm no line cutter so I was about to step to the back of the line when Ms. O'Hara stopped her grandson and spoke directly to me.

"You ought to be part of the family," she said. Without ever having met me before she comes out with a statement like that, in public no less?

"Well, I believe I am."

She paused to look me in the eye. "Do you know it, or just believe it?"

Without hesitation I replied, "Oh, I know it. The rest of the world just doesn't know it yet."

She smiled a big knowing smile and moved on, greeting every one of the hundred or so people who came to see her. I watched her and my resolve was refreshed. If a close friend and leading lady of John Wayne saw the resemblance, even in casual western clothes, and spoke up, there had to be a reason. I never expected that. I never expected to speak with her, but she treated me like family, at least she did until the family got wind.

Later that morning they were breaking ground for the new museum and Ms. O'Hara was having photos taken with men dressed as John Wayne, though none of them looked much like him. Taking charge, she singled me out. "You come over here, you're not getting out of this." I was invited to take photos with her and the others though I was not dressed like The Duke.

Frequent John Wayne movie co-star Maureen O'Hara with the Author

Later I had another photo taken with her with my own camera. That's the only one I have personally. All the photos taken that day are on file somewhere in the museum, except photos of me. That's the kind of prejudice I deal with. I was also pleased to give Ms. O'Hara signed copies of two of my books, "Blood Once Spilled" and "The Treasures Del Diablo" in which I penned, "To the First Lady of John Wayne movies, From the Grandson of The Duke".

That evening they held a dinner and auction, and Ms. O'Hara told some good stories about my grandfather, things I didn't know, since I'd only begun to dig deeper into the mystery. I asked her to sign an old shovel I restored just for that occasion. It was an old wood-stove shovel like the one she was spanked with by my grandpa in the movie "McLintock!". She agreed but noticed I didn't have it with me.

Since the shovel was meant for the auction, I soon retrieved it and once again asked for her signature, then told the fellow to put it in the auction. A few minutes later another fellow brought the shovel back to me and nervously said, "Ms. O'Hara can't be bothered with signing this right now."

I responded that it was for the auction and not for me personally. His curt reply was simply, "Sorry, they refuse to add it to the auction." He hurried away while I just stared in disbelief. I didn't figure it mattered where the shovel came from, only that it would fetch a good price with her signature on it. In defense of the messenger, he was looking up at six feet four inches of John T. Wayne, whose eyes were burning a hole right through him.

That evening I had the pleasure to meet several nice folks such as Roy and Marge Tudor from Madison, Wisconsin; we remain friends to this day. All those at my table were witness to what happened that day, including the shovel incident. Another couple had their daughter Sarah with them, who is now in college. There was nothing to do but shrug it off, yet it seemed I could feel the prick of the knife in my back. It was obvious to all that I was not going to be allowed into the John Wayne family.

I realized the prejudice directed at me included control of anyone or anything surrounding me. It was obvious they never asked Ms. O'Hara to sign. As a memento to remind me of the incident, the shovel hangs in my library where I can see it as I write. It was not the last time I was shunned; it happens more than could be believed. It would be nice if I could be recognized as The Duke's grandson, which would also return my father's heritage, as well.

I can't read what may be on people's minds, but I'm certain there was a conversation on their flight back home to Boise, Idaho. You see, Ms. O'Hara was also accompanied by Aissa Wayne, The Duke's daughter, and my aunt. I had a chance to chat with Aissa that morning as well. I found myself wondering how my appearance triggered such a comment from someone as close to The Duke as Ms. O'Hara.

A few months earlier I visited the Alamo in Texas and picked up a copy of "The Bugles are Silent," by author John Knaggs. John was signing a lot of books that day and he didn't look up when asking how I wanted my copy personalized. I replied, "Just make it to John T. Wayne." Hearing the name, he glanced up, then stood to shake my hand. "Well, I'll be, I guess it is John T. Wayne. Good Lord, you look just like The Duke."

"I come by it honestly," was my reply.

He asked me to wait until he finished with the line of book buyers so we could go across the street for lunch. When he signed my copy of his book he wrote, "To the grandson of the old Duke". From then on, I signed most of my books the same way. It seems only natural.

In 2015 I was invited back to Winterset, Iowa to sign books in the town square. By then I had four westerns in print. I met a lot of people who were surprised that John Wayne could have had a grandson who looked anything like him.

CHAPTER 11
TURNING BACK THE CALENDAR

I recently learned that my grandmother was called by Lettie as a young girl, and she is listed as such in the 1930 census.

1930 Census showing the Author's grandmother as "Lettie".

I loved her a great deal. That doesn't mean I understood her silence. She wore her grandmother's badge very well. If you stopped at her place, you wouldn't leave hungry. Didn't matter what branch of the family you were from.

In 2009, a few months after my father's funeral, I stopped by her Fulton, Kentucky home for a visit and maybe finally get some answers to questions still ringing in my head. I parked across the street from her apartment. It was not uncommon to not see her Buick out front because someone in the family would often borrow it. When I got no answer to my knock I turned to leave and saw her parking at the sidewalk. She wheeled that car like she was twenty-years old. She was, in fact, ninety-two!

Noticing a scrutinizing look upon my face she announced, "I had to go to the store. I know how to drive, and I know where E.W. James grocery is. Been shopping there my whole life. If you want to eat, get the groceries, and bring them in the house." That was more explaining than I ever heard from her.

Later that evening we were going through some family photos she'd had for years when one photo in particular of a beautiful young lady caught my eye. "Who's this, Granny?"

"Why, that's me, silly!"

I was stunned into silence. This was my grandmother? She was drop-dead gorgeous! I may be a bit biased, but the kind of beauty I saw in that picture is usually reserved for angels. The first memory I had of her was that she was advanced in years, with gray hair and nine children. To this day I hardly believe how beautiful she was as a teenager.

But it began to explain a few more things. A normal man would have trouble walking away from such stunning beauty. So now there's no doubt in my mind about what happened. I've seen pictures of John Wayne's wives, his secretary, Marlena Detrick, and a few of his leading ladies, such as Ms. O'Hara. As a teenager, Granny was more beautiful than all of them put together! Suddenly it was no longer a big leap to understand what happened in 1934.

I gave those photos to my aunt for safe keeping. She gave them to another aunt who has since passed away, and now I'm not sure where they are or if I'll ever see them again. But I'll continue to look for that photo until I find it again.

Other than that photograph, I didn't get the answers to my questions when I visited Granny. But it's easy to understand that although her first child was hidden from everyone, she quietly declared her contempt for the cover-up by naming future children as she did.

CHAPTER 12
COINCIDENCE? PROBABLY NOT

I mentioned a few names earlier but here are lists you might find interesting.

John Wayne family names:	Names in my family:
Duke	Duke
John	John
Wayne	Wayne
Marion	Mary Ann
Robert	Robert (Bobby)
Morrison	Morris
Pat	Pat
Melinda	Linda
Mary Antonia	Mary Ann
Virginia	Virginia

It's highly unlikely this was an accident. Every name on the right belongs to my father's brothers and sisters, except the first two, though they are in our family. While Virginia wasn't a family member, she was John Wayne's personal cook for many years. Granny named her children in such a manner as to duplicate the John Wayne family. Was this a way for her to shed her guilt in having never told my father or us boys from whence we came? My father looked just like The Duke, my son and I do, as well; it gives one pause to ponder. An attorney might consider these facts as overwhelming circumstantial evidence.

Those who knew John Wayne's real name, his nickname and his stage name probably see a slight connection.

But consider the more obvious connection. My uncle Wayne Morris was such because Granny left off the last two letters from John Wayne's real name, Marion Robert Morrison, later changed to Marion Michael Morrison. All my life, Uncle Wayne was known as Wayne Marsh, which was probably intended to separate any connection to the Morrison name. It wasn't until his death that I learned of the family's assumed deception, allowing Uncle Wayne to be known as Wayne Marsh, keeping his first name of Wayne.

How does one get Marsh from Morris? Even with a southern accent, I haven't been able to figure that one out. There's no doubt I still have a lot of questions, but, because the truth always comes to the surface, I expect I'll get my answers eventually.

Is your life a crazy jigsaw puzzle? Were you adopted, shunned, or lied to from birth? Then you, too, have an American Heritage. It may not involve John Wayne, or some Hollywood movie star, but this book is named for all of us, every single American who has no idea who their real family is…you, too, have An American Heritage.

CHAPTER 13
JOHN T. WAYNE

I was born in St. Louis, Missouri on August 14th, 1958, and named Terry Wayne Hammock. My father was Billy Gene Hammock, (according to his false birth certificate) and my mother was Bonnie Marie Moore/Hammock. I have two brothers, John Andrew, and William Eugene.

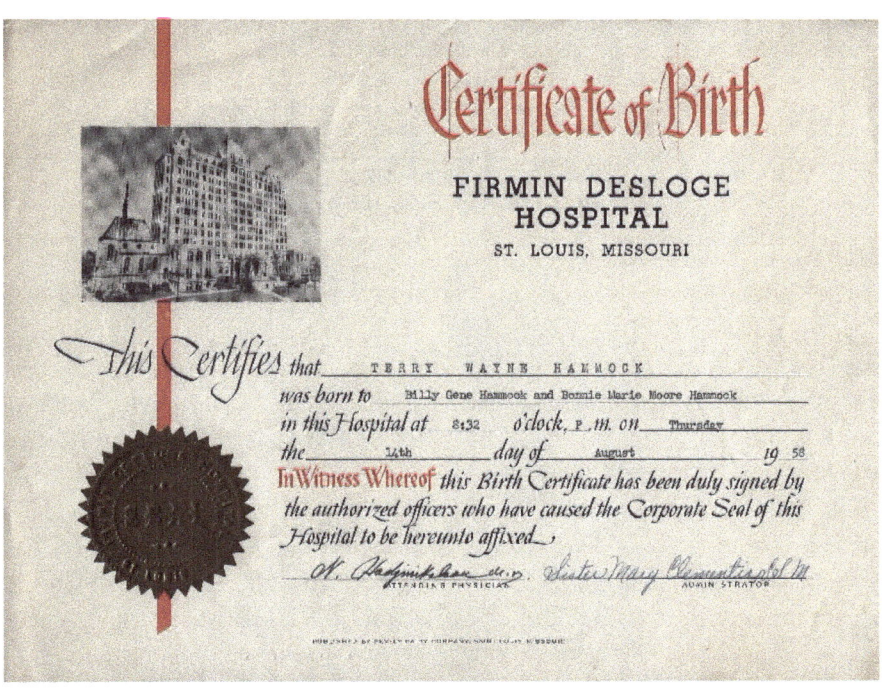

My early days in the 60's was not anything special or out of the ordinary. I was the middle of three brothers living in Big Springs, St. Louis, Joplin, and Independence, Missouri. In those days, my Uncle John was a teenager doing some fun things…at least, I thought so.

The Author's Uncle John and Aunt Sandra

He used to ride his bike by our house at the end of the road overlooking Bear Creek in Big Springs. I admired his bike because it had a small motor attached to it, so he didn't have to peddle when he got up enough speed. He would come by our house just flying, or it looked like flying, to a three-year old boy like me.

Uncle John was the one I looked up to in those days because my dad was spending a lot of time at the hospital fighting Spinal Meningitis and wasn't around much. Johnny Moore was always up to something.

On one occasion I was swinging from the rope swing on a backyard tree when I spied a large snake on the ground where my feet would be in another second. I learned how to climb a swing rope right then, while I heard Uncle John laughing from the corner of the house. I was screaming and crying but not coming down until that snake was gone. After a minute or two John removed the already dead snake, but dad was laughing, too, until mom broke up their fun.

Despite his antics, mostly at my expense, Uncle John was my hero. I learned to be cautious around him and not take everything for granted. A few years later he came to our house in Joplin driving a very pretty blue '63 Ford coupe that sounded loud. At seven years old I didn't know much about such things, so I asked him what he did to make it sound like that.

He opened the hood, twisted off the radiator cap and started pouring water into the thirsty beast. He looked straight at me saying, "You just add water!"

I loved that car because it had the neatest sounding engine. It was sporting something they called "straight pipes". But I soon learned that my hero told me a fib. I watched my dad put water into our car and the sound never changed. I pondered that for a couple of years until I realized that what my Uncle had proposed was impossible. That kind of engagement was most likely what spawned in me a true passion for automobiles.

Now, when it comes to automobiles you don't exactly get to put one over on me. For many years after leaving the Marine Corps I was an ASE Certified Mechanic. My first car was a 1968 Chevelle convertible. I've owned many Chevelles over the years.

Today my Uncle John has a nice collection of old automobiles, from Hot Rods to originals. I still love and respect him. He was a little wild in his younger years, but once he got married and started a family he settled down and got serious about life and raising his family. His son, my cousin Steve, runs the family business now, Moore Cabinet in Trenton, South Carolina. We now all share a passion for Classic American Metal. And, for the record, today I do believe everything my Uncle John tells me.

I also have an Uncle Wayne who is my dad's half-brother. He was a good man and a preacher who always liked a good clean joke. He and his wife had a son and several daughters. He was the one the family always called him Wayne Marsh. He was born in 1941, six years after my father, and was the first child in the marriage of William Alford Gordon and my grandmother Lela. Granny already had one child (my dad) but it seems he was handed over to his grandmother, Rosa Lee Clements to be raised as her own. In the 1940 census my dad is listed as a brother to Lela Pearl Clements. In reality, he was Lela's son. That's how the family dealt with my dad being born out of wedlock.

I was raised as Terry Wayne Hammock. I changed my name legally in 2012 once I became certain John Wayne was my grandfather. I'd been writing since 1985 when I lost my daughter, Kimberly, to cancer, and before I knew of my connection to The Duke. Writing helped ease my pain. I'd never tried publishing my work because I knew the work wasn't ready. You see, I flunked English all through my school years. I couldn't get a handle on the mechanics of nouns, pronouns, verbs, punctuation, and participles. I could speak well, but that doesn't mean I knew how to write a great story. It took a lot of years for my story telling ability to catch up with the stories in my head.

HAMMOCK.Order for Name Change
JTB/amm
8/7/2012
F#12387

FILED
SEP - 5 2012
GREENE CO CIRCUIT CLERK

IN THE CIRCUIT COURT OF GREENE COUNTY, ARKANSAS
2ND JUDICIAL DISTRICT
CIVIL DIVISION

IN THE MATTER OF:

TERRY WAYNE HAMMOCK   PETITIONER

NO. CV-2012- 192

ORDER FOR NAME CHANGE

On this 5th day of September, 2012, the Petition of Terry Wayne Hammock is presented, the Petitioner appearing by and through his attorneys, Branch, Thompson, Warmath & Dale, A Professional Association, and the Court, from the Petition filed herein, the testimony given, and other proof before the Court, doth find:

The Petitioner is the same person as Terry Wayne Hammock which name is in the Certificate of Birth No. 124-58-059189 filed in the office of the Division of Health of Missouri Standards Certificate of Live Birth, and the Petitioner has shown reasonable cause for changing his name.

IT IS THEREFORE, CONSIDERED AND ORDERED that the Petitioner's name be changed from Terry Wayne Hammock to John Thomas Wayne and that the Petitioner shall hereafter be known as John Thomas Wayne; IT IS FURTHER ORDERED that he shall afterward be known and designated, sue and be sued, plead and be impleaded, by the name John Thomas Wayne.

IT IS FURTHER ORDERED that the Petition filed herein and this Order be entered by the Clerk upon the Record of this Court.

A TRUE COPY
I DO SO CERTIFY
JAN GRIFFITH, CLERK
BY _____ D.C.

Name change order allowing the Author to change his name to John T. Wayne

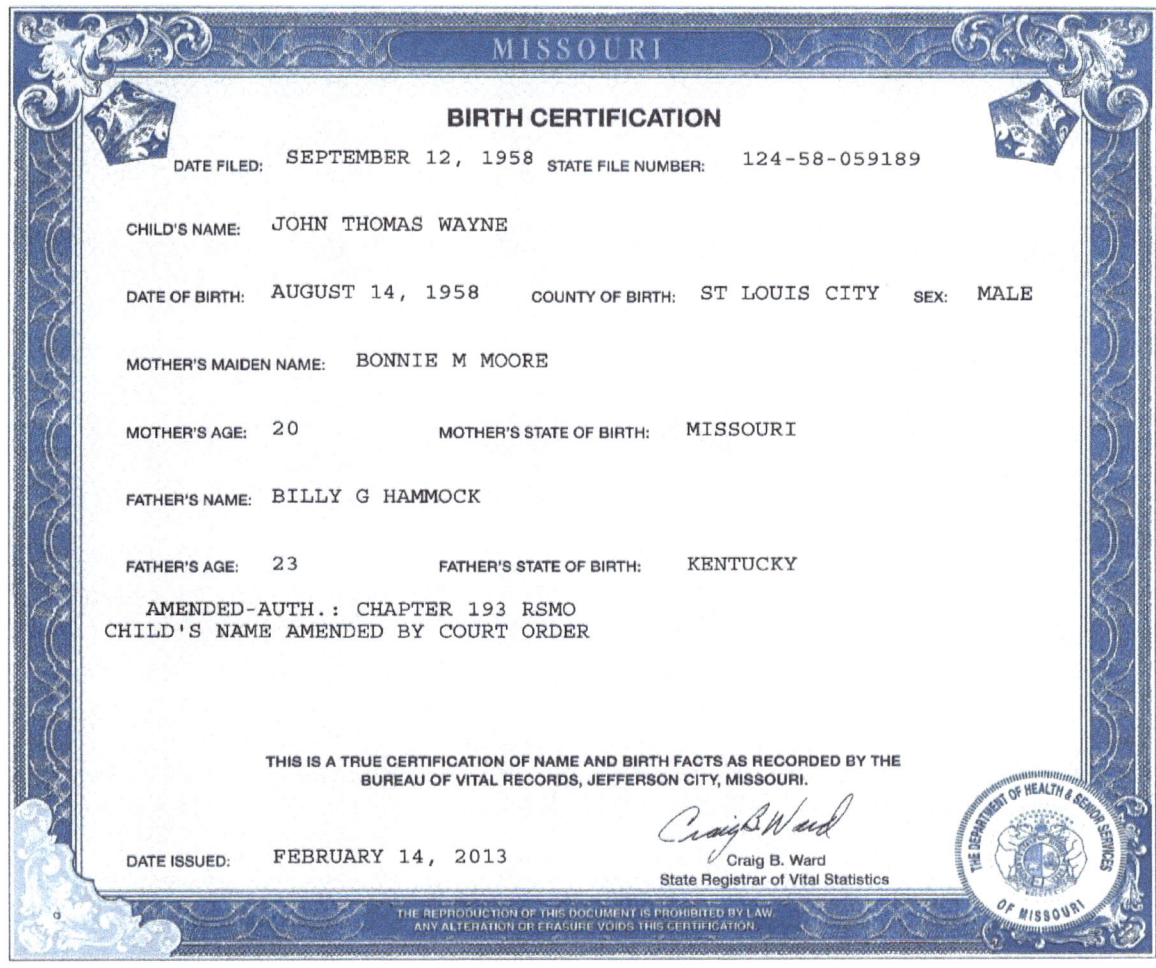

The Author's revised birth certificate with his new legal name "John Thomas Wayne"

What's ironic is I wrote "The Treasures of del Diablo" twenty-five years before I had any idea about my own true identity, yet the book is about a young man who also had no idea about his true identity. He was going through life not knowing he was a Westmorland and heir to a fortune. Isn't life strange? I had no idea, but I was living vicariously through my writing, complaining to God, begging for a solution. I provided one in my book, but who knew that God would eventually provide an answer for my life?

We seemed to move around a lot when we boys were growing up. I think it was because Dad was in and out of hospitals in the late 50s and 60s. Finally in 1965 Dad settled into a job working for Carl Brandley at American Fixture. It allowed him to make a little headway in life. Dad bought his first house in Independence, Missouri. My mother's Uncle

Woody and Aunt Wilma lived across the street. Funny, after fifty years I still remember our phone number as SY6-4086 and theirs was SY6-4081.

About five years later we moved to Hermann, Missouri after our parents split up. Talking with my mother many years later it seemed my father wasn't expected to live when he was born. No doubt Dr. Morrison (AKA Dr. Baker) felt that was the case, though Dad proved everyone wrong.

But knowing that brings me to another question. Who paid all the doctor's bills? The medical bills during his life must have been insurmountable. I never saw him receive a bill or pay one. I learned that early in my dad's life Dr. John C. Morrison offered to teach Dad his profession. Dad declined because doctors made house calls and dad was unable to drive a stick shift car. He only had one good arm and hand, and one leg was several inches shorter than the other. So why did Doctor Morrison take such an interest in my father's future? We'll probably never know, but we do know that Dr. Morrison knew more than anyone alive about what happened at the party at his home in the spring of 1934. Why did he feel beholden to our father?

One summer we lived in Forsyth, Missouri (where Donna and I were married more than thirty years ago). Anyway, dad was preaching at Cedar Creek Church and one afternoon we all headed to town in our ugly green 1970 Dodge Monaco two-door. Dad had become adept at handling that big car in turns, hugging the shoulder stripes in both directions, but never crossing. I'd seen him do it while I was standing in the back of a pickup. I knew right then I wanted to be as good a driver as my father, or better.

Notice my father in the photo below. That was his normal stance when standing still. The tall lanky kid on the left is me, Terry Wayne, at the age of twelve. Dad was pastor of this church!

The Author as a teen (far left) and his father (far right)

Years later, when I came home from the Marine Corps in my SS-396 convertible, I took dad for a ride with the top down. When the automatic transmission shifted into second gear and the tires spun, I asked him what he thought.

"You're just gonna get yourself killed," was his only reply.

I didn't expect that answer. But that was Dad. Tough in his own way. I guess he didn't understand that I was a good driver, and I understood the nuances of driving powerful automobiles.

Another special memory is of us boys having pet rabbits when we were little. We fed them every day. One day my rabbit was gone, and I couldn't find him anywhere. When I asked my mother to help find it, she informed me that we had eaten it for supper the night before. My stomach rolled at the tragedy of having eaten my own rabbit. I cried for a long time but got over it when the rabbits were replaced with a yard full of chickens. I didn't hesitate to catch one so my mother could use a hatchet to chop off its head and let it run around the yard headless. We would chase it until it stopped, then my older brother John would deliver it to mom to be plucked in a tub of hot water.

Brother John was the fastest of the three boys. I came close in size but never had the coordination or his speed. He eventually left a trail of speed records all over the State of Missouri, some of which I believe still stand today. Knowing now about our true heritage explains a lot about my brother. To me he has always been strong, like The Duke. As for me, I was always the timid one until life and the Marine Corps beat me up a bit. Now I stand up and speak up.

The Author with his brothers and mother

One day our yard was empty of any "pets" to put on the table. My dad was once again in the hospital with Meningitis. I watched my mother take a rifle and shoot a squirrel out of a nearby tree for our supper. We were glued to her until that animal was on our plates because it had been alive a few minutes before. It didn't come from a cage, and it tasted a little different, too. I knew right then I didn't want to talk back to my mother. If you have a mom who can shoot supper, clean it, and cook it, all in a few minutes, you ought to think twice about talking smart to her!

The Author with his mother

Because my father was in the hospital a lot in those days, my mother did her best to feed her children. Sometimes feeding the Hammock family was a community effort as well. Dad was renting our house from a fellow named Victor Gloe (think of the movie "Gran Torino" and "Clint Eastwood," that was Victor) at the time. I'm sure there were times he didn't get all the rent, but he never kicked us out. He checked on my mother regularly, as did Grandfather John Oliver Moore.

Today, Victor's son Jimmy and I are still good friends, and we share a passion for Hot Rods. It seems something is always coming up that prevents me from feeding my passion very well. But I've learned to accept what life brings.

Victor never kicked us out of that house, he never bothered my mother for back rent, he stood in the gap when three of John Wayne's possible grandsons would have been homeless. I spoke with him several times after joining the Marines and learned a few things from him. Of note, he built a three car shop up on the hill by his house and when I asked him why, "Why do you always buy the car parts your sons want?" His answer was a simple one; "I know where my boys are on Saturday night!"

Eventually my father's health improved, and he was able to go back to work. It wasn't easy for him, but he soldiered on. Not too many wanted to hire someone who already had physical limitations. As I mentioned earlier, when we moved to Independence, Dad met a man named Carl Bradley, who became a lifelong friend of the family. A consummate pipe smoker, Carl did everything he could to give our father a hand up. He taught Dad bookkeeping, then hired him to do the books at the American Fixture Company. Whenever Carl got a mind to go fishing, we all went.

The Family Fishing

The two men became co-workers and best friends, so when the company transferred Carl to Joplin as the new plant Superintendent, we followed him there. So began our moving from one Missouri community to another. I lost count of the schools we boys attended, and keeping grades up was difficult. We never knew when we'd be moving again. Making friends, though easy enough, was superficial because there was no telling how long we'd be in one place. Looking back now I see I began to shy away from others because I didn't want to explain things to anyone.

One thing I learned growing up was that most people I'd witnessed offered a view into human nature I wanted nothing to do with. I had a natural compassion for others as a young man, and reserved caution when making judgements. Not that I wouldn't make one, I just didn't think I was qualified to judge someone I didn't know who may have been to hell and back before we met. But sometimes you must reserve judgment until you know who the person is. Seemingly nice people get arrested every day and you want to take care not to be connected with them. By the same token, some suspicious characters have some incredible stories to tell, even though you may judge them unfairly. Discrimination for any reason is not part of who I am, though there are some folks I wouldn't care to be around if the law shows up. But friends like Jim Gloe, John Held of the Stone Hill Winery, and many more classmates are lifelong keepers!

For the record, my take on judgment and discrimination is just that—my opinion. It's what I believe and how I live as a Christian and a child of God. I live my life to my moral standards. You won't find any vulgar language in my novels, or in my vocabulary, just for that reason.

Growing up I often wondered why my dad was so touchy, why he had such a short fuse. He may have suspected some of the truth and I now realize it must have been terribly hard to go through life in pain thinking his father wanted nothing to do with him because he was born with Spina Bifida and suffered Polio and Spinal Meningitis. My father's truth is hidden much deeper and covered in many layers of cruel deception.

It wasn't until his death in 2009 that I started digging into the family history in earnest. I learned my great grandfather (my grandmother's father) was John Thomas Clements. My father used the Clements name until he left home at the age of fifteen or so, though he had never seen or knew of his Birth Certificate. The school he was attending in Kentucky said he couldn't start the ninth grade or High School without providing his Birth Certificate. Due to his medical problems, he'd missed a lot of school, so much that they told him he could not continue to attend school. The Birth Certificate now was not the issue, but his lack of attendance. I think we call that heartless today. The school had little compassion for a young man who was already struggling, needed a little help, and they just booted him out!

As I continued to dig, I became convinced that the evidence and circumstances that I uncovered left no doubt in my mind as to the identity of my grandfather. Numerous people who knew my grandfather, and hundreds of people who only knew him from his movies were all in agreement that I looked, acted, and walked just like him, so as evidence began to pile up, and my suspicion grew it became obvious to me there was a connection, if I could just find it.

During the summer of 2012, after uncovering enough circumstantial evidence to rest my case in court, I legally changed my name from Terry Wayne Hammock to John Thomas Wayne. I did it for two reasons: I wanted to claim my true heritage, my birthright if you will, for my father and my children.

I also wrote many western novels over the past thirty years. It was easy to use my first and middle name to publish them as Terry Wayne, dropping my last name of Hammock. With the evidence I'd uncovered I wanted to use my new legal name, John T. Wayne. A few months later, while I was signing books at the Tom Mix Museum in Dewey, Oklahoma, from among the crowd of people someone blurted out, "Good Lord, you don't need a DNA test!"

That seed was planted firmly in my mind. After all, the lies and deceptions were elaborate and complex to protect one man's growing career in Hollywood. There was a lot at stake. I figured the best way to settle the matter was to put science to work. I had a DNA test done.

A DNA test provides a window into one life history. The results tell a story only of the person tested, and they are general as to family characteristics, origins, and history. To make a link to a particular person or family there needs to be another DNA sample for comparison. But, after a few brushes with the Wayne family, no sample of my grandfather's DNA has been provided, nor do I expect it to be. So, I continue to do it the hard way.

Let me be clear: I understand I won't see any of John Wayne's estate, and I wouldn't take it if I could. I inherited a good deal of his good looks and build, I believe, but I'm my own man. I'm a writer and I stand on my own accord, not his. What I do want is the truth to be known, for my father and for my own family, PERIOD.

For the first few years after I changed my name, you could look up John Wayne on the internet. If you clicked on photos, you could find photos of me mixed in with photos of John Wayne, John Wayne Gacy, John Wayne Bobbitt, and many others out there using the name. None of them much resemble The Duke. But now, you guessed it, you'll barely find any photos of me. They have nearly all been removed. In my opinion, it takes money and influence to pull that off, to massage John Wayne's history to be what the movie studios and family want it to be. Then maybe it's just Google giving me my own page. Maybe I've risen to that level. But, massaging the John Wayne image is something John Wayne Enterprises has been doing since 1935, and they've done a good job.

One of the great things about being John T. Wayne is when I'm out signing books, people who met or worked with my grandfather come forward and tell me how they met him firsthand. These stories I just add to my collection, maybe for a future book. But some are a piece of the mystery puzzle bringing light to another dark spot in my hereditary puzzle.

Often, The Duke was criticized for not fighting in WWII. Yet you can't tell me John Wayne didn't serve. He risked life and limb flying all over the occupied Pacific theater without a military escort to entertain Allied troops. The man who did the flying for my grandfather, and lived to tell the story, still lived in Blytheville, Arkansas until recently.

In 2013 I was signing books on the square in Harrisburg, Arkansas. Unbeknownst to me a man stood across the street watching me for about thirty minutes. When things died down a bit he walked under my tent and declared, "There's no doubt who you are."

Not sure what he meant; I took his outstretched hand as he introduced himself. "My name is Ron Miller. I flew the helicopters in the John Wayne movie 'The Green Berets'. I brought you something," he said, then offered me a sack chock full of memorabilia, including a photo of him with John Wayne while on the set of "The Green Berets".

Photo courtesy of Ron Miller

Ron Miller with the Author

Grandpa insisted that he wanted the best pilot the Army had when shooting scenes for the movie. They sent Ron Miller from Lepanto, Arkansas.

We became good friends. He would call me saying, "I got tickets to the rodeo on Saturday night. Can you make it?" or "We're doing a fundraiser for veterans; can you be there?" That sort of thing went on all the time.

As I was driving home from the Western Writers of America conference in Cheyenne, Wyoming in 2017, my phone rang. Another good friend, Minnie Slack told me Ron had passed away and wanted to know if I could make it to the funeral. I drove all night and well into the next day to his funeral service. I was sad to lose a good friend, but glad he would no longer suffer with the brain cancer he fought for over a year.

Minnie Slack has also turned out to be a good friend. She's had me down to Lepanto many times for events like the annual Terrapin races which have been held for the past seventy-five or so years. She also invites me to do fundraisers for the Johnny Cash House and she's had me ride on a float, whether it's a festival or Christmas. When folks from Ireland come by, she makes sure I'm there to greet them. Minnie is always doing for others and knows everybody. She was a moving force behind bringing The Painted House used in a John Grisham novel to Lepanto, and having it reassembled at the end of Main Street. Though he now lives in Mississippi, I understand Mr. Grisham is from Arkansas.

Minnie Slack with the Author

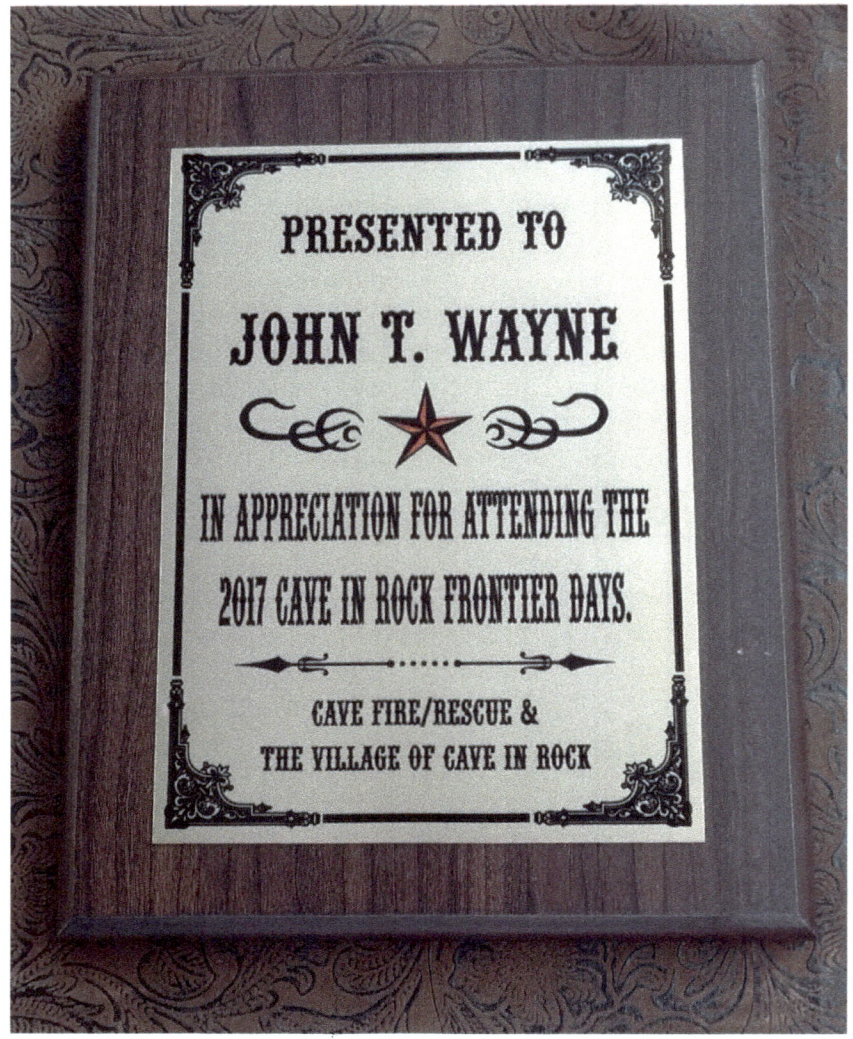

I get to do some truly meaningful things now and then. I went to McDonalds the other day to meet with a family whose son had Down Syndrome. He was eighteen, but he was struggling. John Wayne was his hero. I can tell you I got more satisfaction out of meeting him than he got from meeting me! While visiting with him a woman tapped me on the back and asked, "Excuse me, are you a Wayne?" This kind of thing happens everywhere I go now.

While signing books at the 2015 Memphis Film Festival my friend Christi came to me with a request. "Rex Allen, Jr. wants to meet you." She pointed to a man in a corner with a big white cowboy hat. "The man with the blue shirt and white hat."

Now, the day before, I introduced myself to Robert Fuller (of "Laramie" and "Emergency!" fame) as John T. Wayne, The Duke's Grandson. He looked me up and down and declared, "I'm Patrick Wayne's best friend and I never heard of you."

I said, "Well, now you have."

I figured that was that, until I approached Rex Allen, Jr. My wife was adamant that I go right then to see what it was about, so I strolled over to his table.

"My wife said you wanted to see me," I said.

He leaned back in his chair, crossed his arms and looked up. "Yeah, I want to know what the lineage is." I knew right then that Robert Fuller put him up to it, but I wasn't afraid. I knew what happened and they didn't. Mr. Allen's wife sitting next to him had a look of terror on her face, as if there was going to be a bar room brawl or something.

I stood firmly and looked down at him. "It's real simple, Rex. My father was born in Hickman, Kentucky in 1935 with Spina-Bifida." Before I could take a breath, Rex slapped his leg saying, "I know about that! I forgot all about it. My father told me about that while we were driving across Texas when I was a boy." For the next twenty minutes he filled me in on details about his dad, Rex Allen, and John Wayne. The more he talked the more his wife began to smile. Brawl averted. His story convinced me even more that the people in Hollywood knew all about my father years ago. We just didn't know. The fact is, we were never supposed to know! There was no way those men could have known that our father or his children and grandchildren would look so much like The Duke. Not one of his known family descendants looks much like him. They also didn't suspect that Granny would quietly name so many of her children after The Duke and his known children. The only way I learned of these things was by signing books all over the country. The evidence supporting my case continues to come to the surface, so this story is not over by any means.

As the story becomes more informative over time, I also hear from folks who have a similar life experience with missing pieces. I recently met a young lady who has two young boys in Paragould, Arkansas (there's only one Paragould in the whole wide world). The boys don't know who their grandfather is because their father doesn't know.

I'm learning there are people everywhere, of all ages, who have gaps in their family genealogy. Some know about it but are met with silence, some don't even know it. As a victim of such deception, I can honestly say to those who begin or continue a lie like this, for God's sake and the sake of your family, tell the truth. It isn't right for children to live their lives not knowing or believing a lie about mom or dad or grandparents. Be honest. Admit a mistake. There is time for healing and forgiveness, as tough as that may be. For crying out loud, take responsibility for your own children or mistakes as you may call them. It might be tough for a few family members, but good grief, buck up and be a man, or woman, as the case may be. And silence about a known lie is just as bad as the lie itself. The damage done over time will leave deep mistrust and broken relationships.

I feel like it was providential that my graduation from High School and joining the Marines in 1976 coincided with the last film The Duke ever made, "The Shootist". It's also notable that my grandson, Jeremy Alexander, was born within just a few hours of The Duke's actual birthdate of May 26.

I joined the United States Marine Corps, leaving Hermann, Missouri to board a plane in St. Louis bound for San Diego in 1976. Within five hours I signed on the dotted line and became the property of the United States of America. I was proud to serve my country, but I didn't exactly fit the mold being six-foot-four and 170 pounds. At the end of thirteen weeks, I tipped the scale at 215 pounds, adding forty-five pounds of lean muscle. My mother didn't recognize me when I finally came home on leave.

I left home mostly because I had trust issues. Though the details of my family tree had not come into my life, I grew tired of the lack of cooperation, the silence whenever the subject was brought up. My own mother and father wouldn't discuss it, I had no idea and never dreamed they didn't know. By that time, I figured my brothers and I were never going to know, so we three in our own way just brushed that dirt off our shoulders and moved on.

If you can't trust your own family, who can you trust? There is more family involved here than just mom and dad. At that time, I was pretty certain our grandmother was a key player, and she took her part of the truth with her when she died in 2013 at the age of ninety-five. The naming of her children lends credence to my assumption. Then there is the John Wayne family. Not only did The Duke apparently know of my father, but I also believe some of the Wayne family knew as well. I had to learn The Duke knew about my father from Rex Allen, Jr. at a Film Festival in Memphis, Tennessee. Trust, my foot! Granny was at my father's (her son's) funeral and still she didn't relinquish the truth. And where's the letter written for us three boys?

If this sounds as though things got into my head, they did. The amazing thing is, there was not one ounce of the situation that I could control.

Even though I tried to put the lack of knowledge and truth about our family behind me, the secrecy of it all really messed with my head, at least for a while. People make mistakes, then lie about them, then cover them up so the following generations become part of the deception. They are not given the chance to learn from the mistakes made by their parents, so they become doomed to repeating the same mistakes in their own lives.

I'm reminded of a story of a boy taking advice from his father; "Son, watch where you step in life, there are many traps." The boy replied without missing a beat. "You watch where you step, Daddy, I'm following you."

I've avoided laying a heaping portion of the conspiracy to hide the truth at the feet of Hollywood. By some accounts Josephine had to ask permission from a Catholic priest just to offer her husband, The Duke, a kiss. You can just imagine how well that went over. Their love life was probably limited by priest permission as well, so all was not hunky-dory in the Wayne household.

I remind you of the time in America that John Wayne began his Hollywood life. The country was tired of war, and more of it was looming in the future. The people needed heroes, and they looked to the big new screens to escape, to find hope and pride in those who displayed courage in the face of evil. Hollywood created many of these men and women from ordinary folks like Marion Morrison. They were also incredibly careful and controlling with their images, on and off the screen. Once the fans responded to a particular actor, any negative word or action from or by that actor was bad for the box office and bad for the studios bottom line. John Wayne was a good man who was turned into a superhero who did everything on screen right. On screen you get to edit out the mistakes, off screen that's what was done to my father, he was edited out of the picture.

I understand how difficult it is to be faithful with temptation all around. In my first marriage I often did not get satisfaction at home, so I wasn't beyond finding it where I could. I paid dearly for it in the end. I'm a lot older and wiser now, but back then, after going through the trauma of losing a child, I just wanted to be loved, to be consoled. I made the mistake a lot of young people make. I was confusing sex with love—two quite different things. I know that now. The love and trust of a good woman along with a healthy relationship with our Heavenly Father creates much better results.

I learned some time ago that the two most powerful forces in the universe are both trinities. The Father, Son, and Holy Ghost are number one, and the most powerful, but right behind that is a husband and wife with God at the helm. But beware of the danger if you leave God out of the equation. Look at what's happened to our public schools since removing God from the classroom: they are failing in every way. If you value your marriage, it's good to allow God to be your navigator. Now, put both forces/trinities together, and you can become the most powerful force on Planet Earth, with God's blessing.

As Americans, we can't have freedom without God. The moment you remove God from this nation, it will become a nation gone under. It will no longer espouse freedom for the American people. How do I know that? When the Founding Fathers signed the Declaration of Independence, they were signing a contract with God Almighty, the only nation on earth with such a Contract or Covenant with God. The term Federal in its original form meant Covenant or Contract with God. That definition has been removed altogether from the dictionaries of today. But that does not mean it no longer exists. Thank God He is still honoring that contract that was signed by inspired men, sealed, and delivered all those years ago. Those men pledged their lives, families and fortunes to defend that contract and some of them paid all three. But when the dust settled, we were One Nation Under God, and we still are today. There may be some who do not like that idea, but they haven't the power to change it.

As I said before, after taking my wife's advice I started wearing western clothes to help in promoting my books. I changed my name in 2012 to John Thomas Wayne because of the mystery we lived in growing up, and the constant comments from well-meaning strangers of how I looked so much like The Duke. Digging for the truth added more fuel to that burning fire.

But after two years I couldn't go anywhere without someone saying something. Probably not really coming to complete terms with the loss of two children "primed the pump", so to speak. It was really getting to me, and this old hound dog considered the fact I might be barking up the wrong tree. Nothing made sense. Not knowing who my family was, it seemed impossible that I could be related to John Wayne. I would look in the mirror and stare at photos of him and, try as I might, I just couldn't see what a great many people did. I considered checking out of life again when things began to happen too fast, but I knew from experience that was no answer.

Then I found a photo of The Duke on his boat without his cowboy hat, it stopped me dead in my tracks. It could have been me in every way. Finally, I could see what everyone else was seeing and it shook me to the core. Not long after, I found a photo of Dad, well, it wasn't Dad, it was The Duke, but I couldn't tell him from my own father. It wasn't long before I began to see my brothers, my son, Dad, and myself in photographs of The Duke. This was not troubling, but overwhelming. I couldn't believe this was happening. Now I can watch a movie and imagine my father, especially when he tips the table in "North to Alaska", stampedes across the bridge and crashes the party that was going on. Only Dad couldn't run like that. My father couldn't run at all.

There is something here that I must say. My true heritage is that of being a member of the body of Christ. Once he took over my life, I received his DNA. John Wayne was a man, same as me, he could make mistakes, same as me. My heavenly father is the most important heritage I could have, as He leads me home. The John Wayne heritage comes in second. John Wayne can't save anyone, only our Lord and savior can do that. Anyway, nothing I have learned was of my own accord. God provided me answers wherever I went. I didn't see that coming. I'm thankful that He allowed me to be beat up in life the way He did, He was preparing me for things I had no inkling of. Life is tough, it's even tougher when your rightful family name has been cut from the family tree.

CHAPTER 14
THE SUMMARY

I learned as a young boy that most kids had grandparents: one set with mom's maiden name and one set with dad's name…the family name.

We began to suspect that was not so in our family because our grandpa's last name was Gordon, but ours was Hammock. So, like any inquisitive kids we would ask the simple question, "Who is our grandpa?" We never got the answer to the question, only, "It's none of your business, go play!" Dad wouldn't tell us, and mom didn't know. We learned after my dad's funeral that he didn't know for sure, either.

The next logical step, for any kid who thinks, would be to take the question up the ladder to grandmother. But we got no satisfaction there, either. Even a kid could figure out that something wasn't right with the whole thing, but we were also smart enough to know we didn't want to stir up a hornet's nest.

I learned later that Granny left a sealed letter behind, but its whereabouts and contents are unknown at this time. It also became obvious in my later years that Hollywood had a big hand in the mystery, and they were very thorough in their plan and execution. All they had to do was alter or hide the evidence and keep everyone quiet until they took the truth with them to their graves. It is quite possible that they figured this little problem would take care of itself. Most children born with Spina Bifida back then didn't survive for long. It was a reasonable assumption, only that's not what happened.

It's probably safe to assume Granny gave her word to not divulge the truth. It seems she or her parents made a pact with the good Doctor John C. Morrison, and perhaps The Duke, to keep silent. But Granny was no fool, and she left a solid clue by the names she gave her children. There are probably other clues, but they're buried deep. If you have my faith, you know those clues will eventually come to the surface.

At one time I didn't want to be anything like my father, he seemed to be mad at the entire world and would snap very quickly if us boys got out of hand. As a child I just knew that was wrong! But I didn't know anything about this story, I had no idea what my father had gone through or what he was going through. Today, I have an immense respect and appreciation for him, but the shame of it all is that I can't tell him. He's been gone for some time now. If I was treated like he was, I'd be mad at the world, too. I can't bring him back, but I can make certain the world knows who he was, even if he didn't.

In 1935, the year of our father's birth, Doctor Morrison was, and had been, the only doctor in Hickman, Kentucky since arriving in 1921. As my father was born with Spina Bifida, he was never going to walk tall or stand straight like his father. He also suffered with Polio and later spinal Meningitis. As he grew older the doctor offered to teach him the profession, though I did not know of this until after my father's death. My younger brother learned of this in a conversation with dad and passed it on.

Dr. Morrison served the community for forty-three years, yet there are no journals archived. When an MD stops practicing, it's customary to pass along those records for public information as well as historical value. Yet, in searching the common sources of information there seems to be a distinct absence of information. And being a 32nd degree Mason was no small feat, so there is even more expectation of historical record.

I learned quickly that what you see on the surface can be changed. What can't be changed are the facts buried deep under the surface. When things don't add up, there is probably a good reason. Remember, if you want to know the truth, do the math.

Our father was born in February 1935 to a seventeen-year-old young lady. There were no statutory rape laws at that time. If a girl was physically capable and had grown into her physical maturity, she was considered a grown woman. Granny was absolutely beautiful to look upon, and in my opinion, prettier than any of John Wayne's wives.

We know John Wayne used to fly into the Jerseyville, Illinois airport frequently to mind his cattle interests at the Hondo Ranch. Our father is buried thirty miles from there. John Wayne's grandfather, Marion Mitchell Morrison, is buried in Little York, Illinois. One could say The Duke had connections to the area.

In 2018, while signing books in Louisville, KY, I learned The Duke kept cattle down in Western Kentucky. The folks who live down there have photos of him on their farm. These facts may seem loosely related, but if you look on a map, Jerseyville and Hickman, Kentucky are close. He depended upon his friend Walter Ruby in Kentucky while he also kept cattle at the Hondo Ranch in Illinois.

In the beginning John Wayne was afraid of horses. He didn't want the public in Hollywood to see him practice riding. It was because of this that he coined the phrase, "Courage is being scared to death and saddling up anyway." He had plenty of cattle country to saddle-up on, out of the prying eyes of the press. He had agreed to do several films and being found out as a reluctant horseman would have caused no end of trouble when it came to getting a feature film contract in Hollywood.

A fact we cannot omit here is that there are now three generations (my father, me, and my son Ryan) who look a great deal like The Duke. I have a photo of me from thirty years ago where I'm the spitting image of Clyde Morrison, John Wayne's father. There may be someone out there who looks like any one of us, but five generations who so closely resemble one another shout heredity, not chance.

Clyde L. Morrison (the Author's great-grandfather, source public domain) and the Author c. 1993

Early in John Wayne's career he was known for being one who liked the ladies. A book released in 2012 mentions how he and his friends could play all night and work all day. As time went on, they complained about getting old, not being able to go all night like they did in their younger years. Difficulty at home lends a bit of plausibility to the tales. But Hollywood is quite adept at keeping things under control, and frankly, it's nobody's business.

After my father's funeral in Ferguson, Missouri in the spring of 2009 I learned my Aunt Ann was really Mary Ann. I never knew that. I was closing in on 50 years old when learning this. Her middle and last name is all I had ever known. John Wayne's first daughter was Mary Antonia, called Toni. That's much derived from her Spanish heritage. Mary Ann came into this world many years later, my aunt is younger than me. Then the final child was born to my grandmother, and everyone calls him Bobby. Isn't Bobby a common name for Robert? So, as you see once again another John Wayne name for Granny's last child. Mary Ann was called Ann and still is. I've never met a "Bobby" who wasn't nicknamed from "Robert". For all I know his birth certificate may say Robert. Both children are younger than I, but they are my aunt and uncle. What kind of name deception is going on here? John Wayne's middle name when he was born was Robert as in Marion Robert Morrison. Later when his brother Robert was born, his name was changed to Marion Michael Morrison. Why did my grandmother name almost all her children after John Wayne and his children after my father was born? Dad didn't get such a name, or did he?

I don't know what the court sealed birth certificate says. For all I know it could say John Wayne Morrison. How can my father look just like The Duke and Granny named her children in such a fashion?

Given the moral standards of the time, when a person of stature or power made a mistake of personal weakness, the revelation was often career ending if found out. In the case of John Wayne, a valuable American hero, the options for repairing his mistake were limited to the Catholic Church, the Masons, and Hollywood.

The Catholic Church at that time would go to any length to cover up the birth of a child from an affair with an upstanding church member. An organization based upon sacred vows is very adept at the vow of silence.

The Masons are another organization devoted to secrecy. Doctor Morrison, The Duke, and Walter Ruby were all 32nd degree Masons. It's easy to surmise that men that high in the brotherhood could influence or maintain a conspiracy of deception.

The Morrison link adds more mystery. There are a few unanswered questions concerning his family tree. I don't believe it's a stretch of the imagination to consider Dr. Morrison might be a cousin to Clyde and his brothers, but I haven't been able to confirm such a relationship. I have gotten hints from Ancestry, but all I have learned is that most of the Morrison family names are listed as private and cannot be viewed.

Having a baby with a seventeen-year-old girl while his wife was at home nursing their son Michael would have ended his career in Hollywood if it became public knowledge. I have already stated the obvious financial incentives for Hollywood's part in the conspiracy of deception.

After my uncle died, my Aunt Judy told me that Victor Hammock was my grandfather. My Aunt Ann said spitefully, "Everyone knows Doctor Morrison delivered you three boys." I think what she meant was that he delivered all of Granny's children, including her and Uncle Bobby. We three boys were all born in St. Louis, Missouri.

So here is my question. If dad was not Victor Hammock's son, who was he?

If Victor Hammock was really our grandfather and he was buried in Hickman six months before I was born, why not tell me and my brothers and be done with it? Victor can't talk, he's dead. My dad suspected a lie from reading his Birth Certificate in High School but could never get to the truth. I think he looked just long enough to realize his fake birth certificate was just another lie but had no idea how to prove it.

After Granny died the rest of the family made certain we knew our grandfather was Victor Hammock. They could have told us fifty years ago! But they chose to continue the family lore and ignore the truth. The lies just don't add up and I'm not buying any of it.

So why don't you have a DNA test run? I did a DNA test through Ancestry but all I was able to see off the Morrison name and lineage is blocked, marked private. Ancestry doesn't block out parts of a family lineage without a specific request to do so. It seems someone with influence wants it hidden. What I did find from my DNA test results is parallel to everything we know about John Wayne.

CHAPTER 15
PROOF NOW FINDS ME

Life is full of surprises. You never know what's waiting for you when you leave your home in the morning. Life had to grab me by the neck, shake me for a while, then throw me several times to get my attention. When all of that was happening, I was on the verge of cursing the good Lord above, in fact I did so when Ryan Richard died. But I quickly repented and realized God had nothing to do with death, God is about life. When you realize God is life and offer's eternal life, death no longer has a hold on you.

This, more than anything, is why I hope to stake my claim as John Wayne's grandson.

What happens on this earth is man's doing for the most part. When God sets the path, man cannot undo it, and God set the path for me long before I was ever born, twenty-three years before I was born, to be exact. My father's birth and subsequent cover up was the catalyst for this entire revelation. Once the men of that time covered up his birth, I think God looked down from the heavens and said, "Oh yeah? Watch this!" There is no other way to explain the DNA shared by my father, myself, and my son. My son Ryan from my first marriage looks like the spitting image of The Duke right now.

I have what some folks might consider a weakness: I believe in God.
~John T. Wayne

The Author's children, Kimberly and Ryan

In 2017 a twist of fate brought clarity to years of suspicion when my mother watched the movie "Stagecoach" with Claire Trevor and John Wayne.

Later that evening my mother Bonnie called me. "Can you come over to the house? We need to talk."

"Sure, Mom. Do I need to come now or is the first thing in the morning all right?"

"In the morning it will be fine."

The following morning mom invited me in as always, but before I could ask anything she motioned to a chair. "Have a seat."

My thoughts were racing thinking someone in the family had died. What she told me was something completely different.

"You're right," she blurted out.

I looked at her oddly because I didn't have any idea what she was referring to. "Right about what?"

"You're right about being John Wayne's grandson."

Well, you can bet I was surprised! My own mother had been looking at me like I was crazy, ever since I tried to tell her what I learned and claimed my heritage as a result. Now, here she was agreeing with me, and I was just a little shocked.

"Mom, you've been looking at me funny for a couple of years now. What changed?"

Mom spoke without hesitation, "I was watching 'Stagecoach' last night. I'm telling you, except for the fact that your dad was crippled, I couldn't tell him from John Wayne, especially when he looked up from under his hat. Those eyes are your dad's eyes. This is the same look your father used to give me when he was upset with me. I sat and bawled my eyes out because it finally dawned on me that you were right."

I pulled up an old issue from a few years ago. "Mom, just looking like someone doesn't make you family."

"They lied to your dad. I forgot all about it, because for years after going through the divorce with your father I just wanted to forget him, for years I erased my memory of anything that had to do with him."

"How was Dad lied to?"

"He was told his mother was his sister and used the last name of Clements until he left home to go live with your Uncle Buddy in St. Louis. That's where I met him."

You don't marry a man without knowing a little of his life's story. She knew of the difficulty her husband had as a teenager with the Clements family name. For reasons only known to them, my parents bitterly ended their marriage in the early seventies. Mom spent many years trying to purge memories of my father from her life, and she did a good job. That is, until she watched the movie "Stagecoach".

Remember, she now has two sons named "John". Isn't that funny! I was just asking how someone names two sons "Bill"? Both Mom and my wife of thirty-plus years finally call me "John T.", which is what I prefer. "John T." is the correction in my family tree, a correction made by me once I was convinced there was no doubt. I wasn't named John; I took the name!

I had a book signing and history lesson scheduled by my PR Manager, Angela, at the Swift Museum in Rogersville, Tennessee which had been abruptly canceled the year before when Anita Swift learned I was coming there to speak.

For more than fifty years Anita Swift had always been known as The Duke's oldest grandchild, at least until the applecart was upset. I can understand how upsetting it must be for someone she has never met to suddenly claim to be the oldest grandchild. But some things just can't be helped. I believe my older brother is the oldest grandchild, which moves Anita to 3rd. Things will get cleared up in due time.

In 2014 I signed books at the Swift Museum. I was sitting in the dining room of a genuinely nice historic hotel where American presidents have stayed, when from behind I hear, "They have a problem, don't they?" The comment came from Stella Gudger, who I learned was convinced not to bring me in for speaking engagements because she had been told I was not The Duke's grandson.

Not sure of her meaning I asked, "Who has a problem?"

"The John Wayne family," she replied, taking a seat.

Stella Gudger was a complete stranger whom I'd never met, yet the moment she saw me, from behind no less, she knew I had to be of the John Wayne family, and she'd been led to believe differently. She saw the same thing Maureen O'Hara saw, and others too numerous to name.

Another family with a similar story on the west coast has contacted me, so it could be that there are even more of The Duke's grandchildren out there. They wish to remain anonymous for now.

Now, you can agree that by chance, there can be lookalikes for any of us. But there is no discounting genetics. I inherited my likely grandfather's genes which have given me everything he was, including many of his thoughts and opinions on life, as well as his looks and mannerisms. God certainly had a hand in how things played out.

Just as I need to know who my grandfather was, my children and grandchildren need to know who their grandfather is. It is for them that I continue the search for the truth.

In 2017 I was signing books in Trimble, Tennessee when Virginia Parks Williamson invited me to the local library on the town square where she grew up. A friend or relative of hers came and bought every book I had. She went home and told her neighbor. It turns out the neighbor, Doug Hay, had a saddle he'd inherited from his friend Jimmy Payne of Dallas and was a big John Wayne fan.

So, one day I received a phone call. The voice on the other end said, "I have something that belongs to you."

Now, I've gotten some strange phone calls over the last few years, but this one was mysterious. I asked who was calling.

"My name is Doug Hay. I have your grandfather's parade saddle. You need to come get it."

"Who is this again?" I asked.

"Doug Hay. I live in Collierville, Tennessee. I've been downsizing lately, and I no longer have the space to keep it. It's yours if you'll come get it."

I live only 85 miles from Memphis, and Collierville is another twenty miles. We made the arrangements, and he gave me the saddle as promised. It turns out the saddle did not come directly from John Wayne, but at one time he owned it and used it in parades.

To this day I have not handled it with bare hands. Gloves are mandatory, because no matter how many signs you hang on things, folks can't keep their hands off. It sits right where it's going to stay, in my personal library.

Saddle used by John Wayne, now owned by the Author.

CHAPTER 16
THE WILD GOOSE

My friend Glen Hale is a Cherokee living in Alabama and about twenty years my senior. I met him a few years ago and he told me a unique story which I feel obliged to share.

Glen Hale was serving in the US Navy on a minesweeper in the late fifties.

While Hales' ship was docked, a Yard Oiler (YO) was making a sweeping turn in the crowded harbor when it crashed into the mine sweeper and nearly sank the ship. The Navy quickly secured the sweeper and put it into drydock until it could be repaired.

Once the repairs were made, the ship was decommissioned and sold to John Wayne, The Duke of Hollywood, who renamed it *The Wild Goose*.

John Wayne's "The Wild Goose". Source Public Domain

I would love to sail on that boat with my friend Glen Hale one day. He would relive a memory and I would have a new one to enrich my life's story.

Everyone has people they've met who lend a helping hand. One of those for me was my good friend Eunice who ran a sale barn in south Jacksonville, Florida off Philips Highway. When we met, I was hauling heavy equipment during the week, but I was always home on Saturday and Sunday to help at the barn. I worked for free if she would let me pick out a few books from her book collection. A fine relationship began that lasted several years. I soon learned that if any of the books had pictures in them, she wanted to keep them. She couldn't see to read or maybe she couldn't read, but she liked to look at old pictures.

There were ten cabins around the barn, and two of them were filled with old books. For the next few years, she helped me build an incredible library of books written before 1900. I quickly learned that in those days when you wrote a non-fiction book you had to tell the truth, or they'd take you out and hang you. Eunice understood my passion for learning. When she passed away, I thought that was the end of my book gathering, but a few months later I received a call from her son who was a professor at Berea University in Kentucky. "We have a complete mess on our hands down here at the barn. If you don't want these books, we're going to throw them out."

Since it was Saturday my answer was, "Don't throw them out, I'll be right there."

I hauled three truckloads of books out of there that day. Some were not in good enough shape to keep and ended up in the trash. But I saved almost all of them and they make up most of my personal library in my study. You never know what you'll learn from old books.

I learned the term "cowboy" was used one summer in 1070 AD in Ireland, and again in 1690 when a herd of cattle was moved from the swamps of Florida to near Atlanta with the help of young boys. No one used the term "cowboy" again until the Civil War when it appeared like magic. I discovered that the orphans from the war became the American cowboys we know and love today. Orphans from the Civil War; who knew?

That sort of woke me up! I began to change all my work to a series called "The Gaslight Boys", the boys who had to live on the streets under the gaslights to survive the war. Once the war had a full head of steam, ranchers all over the country could no longer hire good Cattlemen, Drovers, Wranglers, or Hands since all the men went off to fight on either side. With no other choice the ranchers began to hire orphans off the street and began calling them Cowboys. The term was derogatory at first. I found this in 2010 in Old Town San Diego in the barn loft while visiting my son Beau. It confirmed what I already knew.

The Definition of Cowboy: "Tall in the Saddle"

Only after the Civil War did the term "cowboy" come to signify anyone who tended cattle in the West. Saddles, clothing, and terminology varied between regions and generations. But there were two things all cowboys had in common: hard work and primitive conditions. The average man called himself a "cowboy" for no more than around seven years before settling in town, on his own spread, or drifting on to something else.

Contrary to popular image, the cowboy's life was bitterly hard, and often, very lonely. He earned little, had no permanent home, and was without family, all facts which kept his status low. (Source: Old Town San Diego Museum)

The Author on horseback

When life settles down a bit, I plan to read all the books in my library. I plan to continue writing for the rest of my life, so reading is required. Historical accuracy is necessary, and the best place to find knowledge and inspiration is in those old books. I have first editions of books by Winston Churchill and Charles Dickens, and more than one copy of Uncle Tom's Cabin, circa 1850, has passed through my hands. My books are most valuable to me as research tools, simply because you can't find the information found in them anywhere else. Libraries are always purging their old to make room for new, but I prefer the old. Before our time of modern media, books and newspapers were all we had, and they had to be checked and double checked before a publisher would release them.

Early in my writing career, before I became committed to recovering my true heritage, I wanted to write Westerns. I learned that required knowledge of the Civil War as the foundation for the historical context of the untamed West was a must. There are over sixty-two thousand books written about the Civil War and the men who fought in it, but no mention of the orphaned children left behind. One can surmise that the Federal Government knew they had an orphan problem when the war was over, they just didn't want to get beat up about it. The order was given to Generals in charge to not allow newspapers to write anything that had to do with the orphans. Constitutional amendments notwithstanding, keeping it quiet would take away the issue. Today you can go back through old newspapers and find only veiled mention of something like, "A child died on the street yesterday." The editors could not say it was an orphan leftover from the Civil War, we were under Martial Law. But books were another issue, not so easily controlled.

My wife and I moved to Arkansas from Jacksonville, Florida in 2010. I feel the move put us closer to where some of the truth is hidden at a time when I struggled with my identity as never before. I could have run to a councilor to whine and cry over being a victim, or I could dig deep for the John Wayne courage within, pull on my boots and hat, and go find the real story.

Eunice was a good friend with an incredibly dry sense of humor. She told me often, "I won't tell you something I don't know." She told me that many times before it finally sank in. Of course, she wouldn't! Sometimes I can be a little slow to catch something delivered with such a wry sense of humor.

My Uncle Buddy (grandma's brother) was like that. When he returned from World War II, he went to work building bridges all over St. Louis. When he retired the company brought him back a few months later because the four college students they hired to take his place couldn't fill his shoes. They managed to bring every job the company had to a halt, waiting for steel or supplies not ordered in a timely manner. Uncle Buddy took one man under his wing and worked another two years training him to take his place. The man had been with the company for several years but didn't have a college degree. Uncle Buddy said he had common sense and a willingness to learn.

I've met so many good folks since changing my name to reflect what I believe is my true heritage; people like Darby Hinton, Buck Taylor, Stuart Rosebrook (the editor for

"True West Magazine"), Tim Harris of Memphis who only wants the best for his two daughters, Elvis Presley's nurse, Ron Miller, the grandson of Tom Mix, Gordon Hill, Roy Roger's daughter and granddaughter, and Alison Arngrim (Nellie from "Little House on the Prairie") are just a few. I have friends all over the U.S.

The Author with Julie Fox Ashley Pomilia (L., Roy Rogers granddaughter) and Allison Arngrim

One problem with being invited to sign books is travel. With that comes expenses, hotels, and coordination. No doubt, there will be a lot more in my future. But the problem for me is I hate flying. I don't have the patience for all the rules and procedures, documentation, rental cars, meals and so on. I gave up flying over thirty years ago. The new systems make crime suspects out of innocent American Citizens and I don't care to see a jail cell for any reason. So, I drive if I need to go somewhere. I have a few million accident-free miles under my belt, and the road gives me time to think, to sort out stories I'm working on, or spend some time with The Lord. If the Federal government that buried the orphan problem in 1865 or brought us to this recent COVID fiasco ruins my travel plans, well, I'll just stay home and write.

Early in my search for the truth I would lose some of my resolve. It was easier to believe the lies than spend time running into dead ends. But a lot of things happened when I put on western boots and a cowboy hat. I couldn't leave it alone after that, even if I wanted to.

That realization came to me one day as I was driving out of Texas. Stopping in Laredo for breakfast, I had a waitress who insisted I looked just like The Duke. Later that day, in West, Texas, I had another waitress tell me, "If you had an eye patch, you'd look just like Rooster Cogburn." This was before the recent remake of True Grit. Again, later that evening. I was in Denton, Texas when a young lady came to help me look for a new shirt.

"How can I help…OMG, it's you!"

"Excuse me?"

Pointing to a large-sized poster of John Wayne, she said," That's you!"

At nineteen she didn't know who The Duke was, only that I looked like the guy with his dog in the poster for the movie "Hondo". As you might guess, when I left Texas that day, I was struggling with what to do next about finding my identity.

At the same time the Wayne family was preparing to auction off several items from The Duke's filmmaking days. There was a photo of him in their advertisement which even I couldn't tell from my own father. The photo was of him on his boat fishing with Ethan. My father didn't like being in photographs, but I now have photos of The Duke which reinforce the likeness.

The Author's parents

Photo courtesy "The Dixie Pig" restaurant, Blytheville, Arkansas

As I said, driving gives me time to think. It was then that I heard an inner voice telling me, "I'm trying to tell you dummy, you're John Wayne's grandson." Now, I had prayed to God many times in my life, but all the conversations appeared to be one-sided. I know they were not, because He answered my prayers by doing something in my life. But I'd never actually "heard" an answer. And He called me "dummy", which was an accurate way to get my attention. More than once I'd thought of myself as a big dummy.

For the next three days, while driving over the country carrying out my paying job, I had an incredible argument with God. My mind raced from one argument to the next, finding it incredible that I could actually be John Wayne's grandson. Then it hit me. Have you ever won an argument with God? That was the day I lost the biggest argument of my life. Every objection I threw out was wiped off the table at the speed of God. "You know that isn't true," He would say, then proceed to explain. If you ever have an argument with God, be prepared to lose. He explained everything about my father perfectly. He told me why my father was the way he was, and why we didn't know. Dummy was right!

This happened after Dad, Uncle Wayne and Uncle Russell died. As I said earlier, my Aunt Judy told us that Granny left her a letter to us three boys, not to be opened until after her death. After my conversation with God the wheels started to come off the family wagon full of lies.

I wanted answers right then. I wanted to know why all the secrecy and games, why can't we just know the truth? We were being treated like we were young children who might get our feelings hurt by the truth. We were grown men who had lost children to cancer and suicide and had grandchildren of our own for crying out loud. What's the big stinking secret?

At that time, I had no proof other than a letter I didn't have. I didn't know if the letter would answer any questions, and I still don't. No one in the family has produced the letter and I'm now being told by the family, calling ME a liar and a fraud, that there is no such letter. Well, somebody's lying and it was never me. I had nothing to lie about! Still no answers at all.

After dad's funeral, I went to City Hall, the newspaper, and the library in Hickman, Kentucky where I discovered a few interesting things, most of which I've detailed for you earlier in this book. Now that God answered a lot of questions, pieces of the puzzle began to fall into place.

This led me to move ahead and publish my first book, "Catfish John - The Anatomy of a Bottom Dweller", as John T. Wayne in 2011.

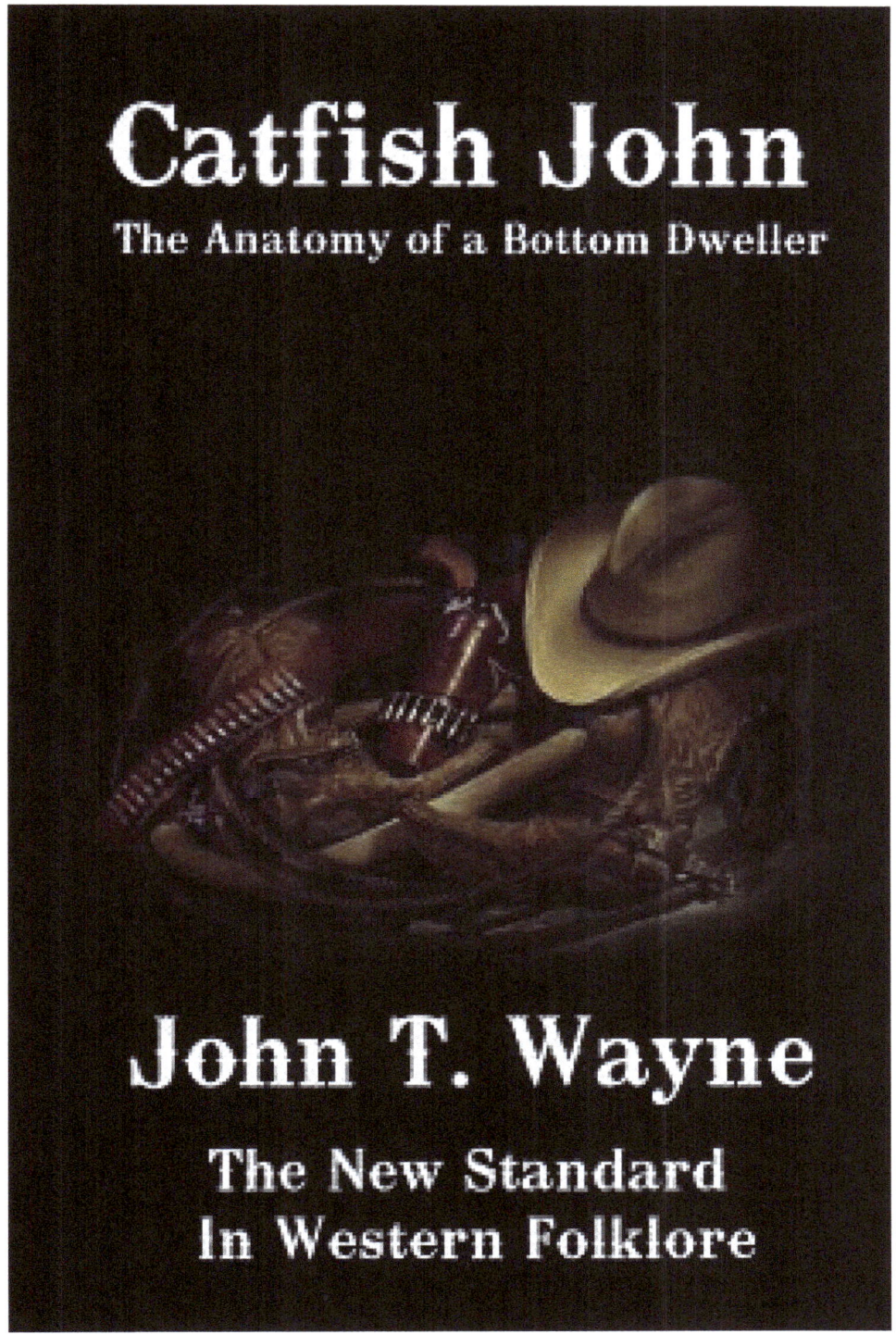

Another solid western fiction from Wayne

Mark Rhodes
Book Reviewer

"Catfish John, the Anatomy of a Bottom Dweller" is Wayne's first novel in the Gaslight Boys series based on the adventures of boys that were orphaned after the Civil War and grew up on the streets of St. Louis. The name gaslight boys comes from the gas streetlights used in St Louis at that time. In this historical fiction novel Wayne takes us back to life in the New Mexico Territory of the old west. Wayne has really done his research on this period of history and painted a very realistic picture of the time. The novel is a first-person narrative told through the eyes of the main character, Rassie Cohen.

Wayne does an excellent job of weaving many old west legends in to this novel. The title of the book refers to the gunfighter Catfish John AKA The Catfish Kid who gained notoriety from a gunfight in Tusosa, Texas in 1886. Other notable old west characters included in the novel are Lem Woodruff, Charlie Emory, Louis Bouseman and Ned Dillon who make up Catfish John's gang. We also see appearances from Wild Bill Hickock, Black Jack Ketchum and General George Custer.

This story reminded me of cross between The Lone Ranger and the Gunfight at the OK Corral. It begins with our hero Rassie Cohen being thrown off the westbound train in middle of the New Mexico Territory. He makes his way to Clines Corner, a small train stop, and proceeds to save Emma, the girl of his dreams and soon to be wife, from the outlaw Catfish John. In the process, Rassie becomes the U.S. marshal for the territory.

They say opposites attract and that is a true statement in the case of Rassie and Emma. They are about as different as two people can be. Rassie is a 17-year-old street-smart orphan from St Louis whose main goal is to find his next meal and stay alive. Emma, on the other hand, is a wealthy educated lady who grew up not wanting for anything. Because they are so different they are both able to learn from each other and they make a formidable couple.

Catfish John is an evil man and has murdered Emma's father hoping to get his gold mine. After Rassie saves Emma a feud ignites between the two, and Catfish John spends his days devising different ways to try and kill Rassie throughout the New Mexico Territory and Texas.

Rassie would like to kill Catfish John but accepts the fact he must play by the rules of the law now that he is a U.S. marshal. He quickly learns that Catfish John will stop at nothing to keep from hanging and Rassie must be on the lookout for trouble at all times if he wants to stay alive.

Rassie, being a new U.S. marshal, has a lot to learn and with the help of Emma and other good people he meets throughout the story he slowly builds a reputation as a lawman. The biggest help to him is his deputy Medicine Cloud, an Indian who becomes Rassie's best friend. Medicine Cloud teaches Rassie many important lessons about surviving out west and saves him more than once on their adventures together.

Wayne has many subplots interwoven into the novel. Many of Rassie's friends from St. Louis come out to join him in the New Mexico territory where they help him and Emma build their dream house and start a ranch. We also get an inside look at the life of Apache Indians as Rassie and Emma spend time with them and recruit the leader Gray Bear to hunt grizzly bears that have been attacking the people of Santa Fe.

This book will appeal to anyone who enjoys westerns and historical fiction. Wayne does a good job developing his characters, but all the background information provided causes the story to drag in parts. The main plot is based on the feud between Rassie and Catfish John and the story gets a little long with Catfish John getting arrested, breaking out and trying to kill Rassie over and over again. I think Wayne could have done a better job of portraying this scenario or broken the story into two books of the series. Wayne does close the novel with a surprise ending I did not see coming. I hope Wayne's continues to write about the adventures of Rassie Cohen. I give this book a B-.

Catfish John, the Anatomy of a Bottom Dweller is available at Publish America, Barnes & Noble and Amazon from $15.95 to $29.95. Mr. Wayne lives in Delaplaine and you can learn more about him at his website www.facebook.com/john.t.wayne.3.

© 2011 The Paragould Daily Press

The following year I published my second novel, "The Treasure Del Diablo". With renewed energy and clarity in my mind I followed that with "Blood Once Spilled", "Ol' Slantface", "Captain Grimes", "Showdown at Scatter Creek", and "Peace in The Valley" (published by Mockingbird Lane Press).

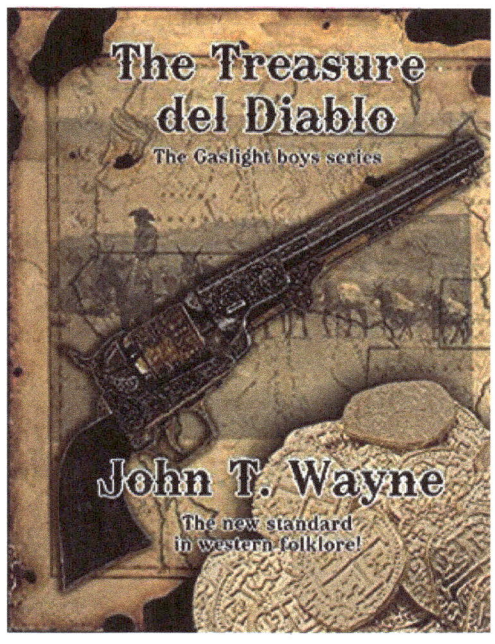
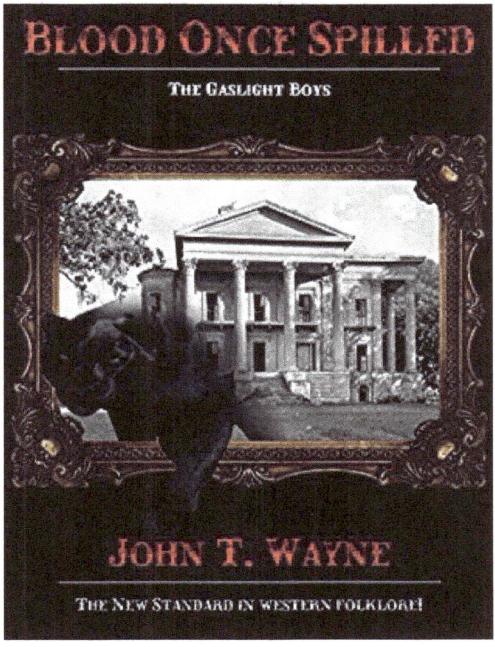

1010 HWY 77 NORTH, POST OFFICE BOX 459, WEST MEMPHIS, ARKANSAS 72303, 870/735-1010 FAX 870/735-1020

May 31, 2017

Dear Mr. Wayne,

Please find enclosed a copy of my book review of *Captain Grimes Unreconstructed*. Thank you very much for sending it to me and for being a part of the city's Sultana Heritage Festival.

I really enjoyed the book. As a historian myself and a Civil War buff, it was fun to read about Mark Twain and Captain Grimes. I did not know who Captain Grimes was, but I did know who Robert Louden was, although you threw me when you introduced him as Bobby. I thought, 'is that the same Louden who invented the coal bomb?' There is a scholar who believes that Louden planted a coal bomb in the Sultana. While I do not believe that to be the case, it was still interesting to learn more about Louden's exploits. I also enjoyed Captain Grimes's side adventure to Van Buren, Mo. I had a girlfriend who is from Van Buren so I recognized the area right away.

Anyway, I am definitely a fan of your Gaslight boys series and look forward to Part 2 of *Captain Grimes Unreconstructed*. As you may know, Marion is working on raising money for a permanent Sultana Museum. I hope you will continue to keep in touch and perhaps even join in our effort. I run across you at festivals every now and then and will say hello the next time we cross paths.

Again, thank you for the book and for being a great American!

Sincerely,

Mark Randall

Mark Randall

One of the hardest parts of this evolving story is the effect it has on people I love: my mother, my wife, my brothers, and many of my friends of many years. I've had to explain many times about the things I've uncovered for them to realize I might be telling the truth. Their skepticism has affected me as well. There are a few family members now who hate me for dragging Granny's name through the mud, even though she was a sixteen-year-old victim, doing what she was told.

I don't blame any of this on Granny. She might have been a victim from the git-go, but no one knows. She may have gone willingly, which seems more likely, but if that's the case, she still became a victim of her own decision. I don't blame her for wanting to spend an evening with The Duke. He was already a well-known actor of the time.

For my part, I just want some justice for my father. He is the one who suffered all the indignity of being born out of wedlock, being born as a throw-away child, one nobody wanted, an inconvenience to all. He deserved better. Imagine being told that you are too old to attend further classes at school because you were in the hospital and missed too many classes!

The Author with Johnny Crawford (Lucas McCain on "The Rifleman")

CHAPTER 17
JOHN WAYNE'S "SECOND SON" DIES

In the spring of two-thousand-nine we lost our father, Billy Gene Hammock. Dad managed to live an amazing seventy-four years when he was only expected to live a short life. Now, that's True Grit right there! He was his own man because there wasn't anyone else for him to trust. My father turned to God, and I don't believe God ever let him down. There was no true family history for him to learn. Ancestry.com didn't exist, nor did DNA tests, no real father figure beyond his grandfather, John Thomas Clements on his mother's side. To my father, Victor Hammock was just another lie. Dad was never part of the Hammock family of Hickman, Kentucky.

Knowing my father, the way I do, it's amazing he didn't go postal on the whole family at some point. And I thought it was hard not knowing my grandfather or even what his name might be. When I think of dad, I'm almost ashamed of myself, not wanting to be anything like him. Guess who I am now? I'm just like him.

When I look at how my son Ryan mimics my own father without being aware of it, it's hard to believe they were rarely together. Ryan met my father when he was three years old, the time we buried his sister in 1985. He never saw dad again. I get to see things my father didn't know, like how gene's work. Ryan has my dad's and my grandfather's genes, their mannerisms, their outlook on life. For some reason, John Wayne DNA knows how to man up!

But everyone is gone now; The doctor who delivered my father, my grandmother, my assumed grandfather (John Wayne), and now my dad. Everyone who had everything to do with the original cover-up is gone or silenced by time. The existing Wayne family has become adept at controlling the John Wayne legend and anyone who attempts to set the record straight is blocked or stonewalled.

I'm not asking a single person to make up their mind right now, because the story is still unfolding. I made up my own mind several years ago because there is too much circumstantial and historical evidence to ever believe the family conspiracy of silence didn't happen. As more is discovered, it advances our family story ever closer to the truth. Even with the court sealed birth certificate, until the Morrison family names are unlocked on Ancestry.com and made public, or a DNA sample is provided by the Wayne family, there will still be questions. I know that, but then again, life is strange, so strange it is almost unbelievable sometimes.

I have presented many facts to be considered, some of them incredible. While we move forward as a family, I only want our true heritage to be acknowledged and a chance to be the successful author I planned to be. I am that man now, for I write novels which I hope will be enjoyed for years to come. As far as gaining my true heritage, the John Wayne family owes me nothing, they didn't do this anymore than my brothers and I did. I still believe in the common sense of the American people. This story may not end in my lifetime.

I know releasing the results of my search for the truth so far will be hard for the American people, and many of the John Wayne fans around the world. Some won't believe the truth unfolding in this crazy life of mine, especially for many of his diehard fans. I admit the entire chain of events is confusing, but I and my family are entitled to the truth. The lies and deceptions have hurt many people, when the truth at the outset would have been dealt with, accepted, and mistakes forgiven. Nowadays, with the entertainment industry seeming to revel in the poor behavior and indiscretions of its public icons, what's the point?

This book is going to be scrutinized by many folks all over the world, but I assure you, while you may find something I don't know about yet, you won't find anything to undo what I know so far. The name Hammock was bogus from the beginning; my father isn't related to any of the Hammocks from Hickman Kentucky. Neither am I.

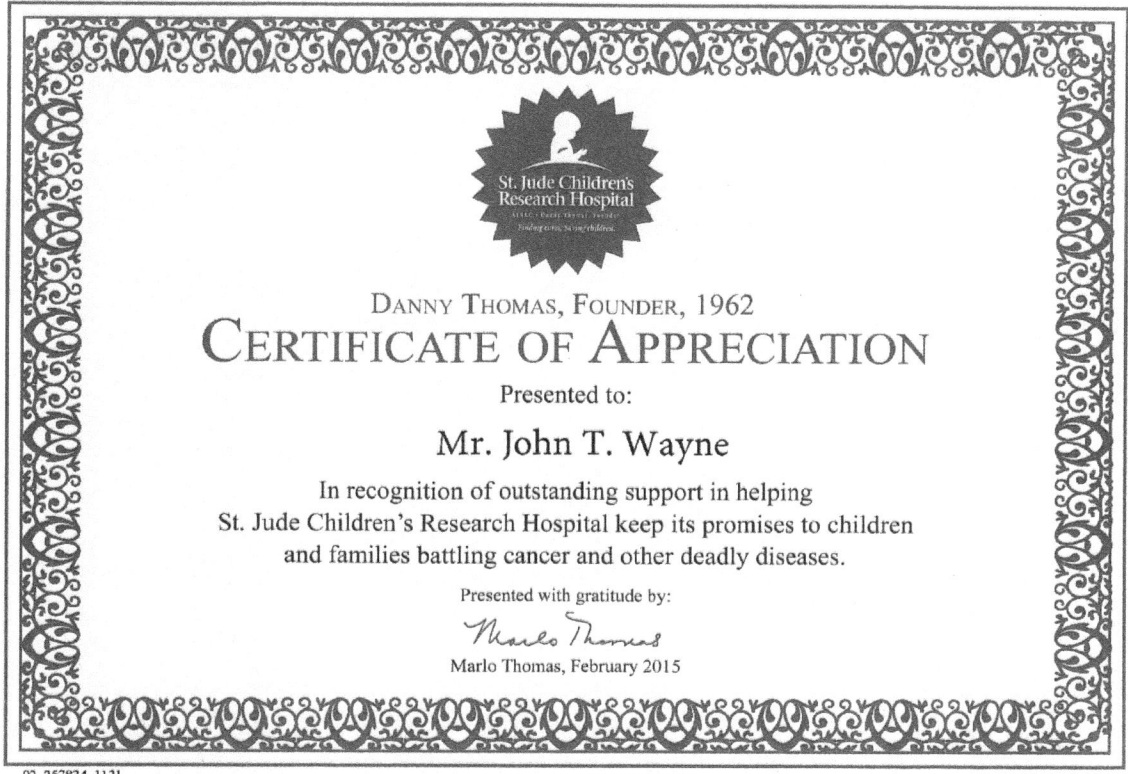

So now you know what I know. The evidence, in pieces, may be circumstantial. But taken as a whole and coupled with God's confirmation, there isn't much room for doubt.

In writing I find happiness. In accepting the clarity and validation of God's message to me I accept the long hours and endless miles to share my work and history with friends and fans. I continue to meet people who share my belief of my ancestry and I never tire of the encouragement and best wishes they bring to me. I return their kindness any way I can.

Knowing the truth is out there, I continue to search for what remains. I hope to uncover who engineered the cover up. Was it my great-grandparents who hid the truth from the family? Was it Hollywood, the Masons, or the Catholic Church? It's possible they all played a part in this cover up. I also understand that the truth will float to the surface when it's time.

Being asked to become part of the True Grit Trail has offered me the chance to live two of my life passions, classic cars, and history. I believe the 2020s will be good years, and by the time this book is finished we will be driving the next annual True Grit Trail Drive. If you have a hotrod or classic car, please consider joining us as we leave from Dardanelle, Arkansas.

March 20, 2019: Arkansas Governor Asa Hutchinson signing the bill officially naming "The True Grit Trail"; the Author is in the white hat.

The Author with Arkansas Governor Asa Hutchinson

The Author unveils the True Grit Trail road sign.

CHAPTER 18
LIKE "GRANDPA", LIKE "GRANDSON"

In 2021 I took part in the independent film "Letters Home", playing the role of Colonel James Chalmers in this Civil War-era movie. According to IMDB.com, this movie was due to be released in 2022 but has yet, at this writing, to be released. The story is about "two young men who are drawn into an adventure that leads them into a war they want no part of" (source: IMDB.com). Filming took place in several areas of Illinois.

John T. Wayne
From the movie, Letters Home.

EPILOGUE

I'm also reserving a good bit of this year for finishing two more books in the Captain Grimes series. Grimes was Mark Twain's best friend, and they joined the Civil War together. In 2024 we'll also be putting the finishing touches on the first books in the True Grit Trail series which tells of the U.S. Marshals working out of Fort Smith.

There's a lot yet to accomplish, but I'm looking forward to meeting Duke fans who are interested in our family history, such as it is. The ending has not yet been written because I will continue to hoard every scrap of evidence I come across, the proof of our true AMERICAN HERITAGE.

To sum things up in "The Duke's own words" as shared by Pilar, his third wife, "Each of us is a mixture of some good and some not so good qualities. In considering one's fellow man, it's important to remember the good things, and to realize his faults only prove he's a human being. We should refrain from making judgments—just because a fella happens to be a dirty rotten SOB."

I hope this book has provided enough information to prove my true American Heritage; if not, it should at least open the discussion as to what happened that night some nine decades ago in a small town in Kentucky overlooking the Mississippi River…

THE WHITE HOUSE
WASHINGTON

Thank you for your kind words and thoughtful gift. Melania and I deeply appreciate your support. We are honored to serve a country that we love and to work every day to improve the lives of the American people.

Your encouragement, and that of millions of Americans, sustains us each step of the way. By working together, we will deliver on the promise of America for all of our people. We will strengthen our national spirit and ensure that America continues to shine as a beacon of freedom for all of the world to see.

We are grateful for your generous gift and support. God Bless America.

Sincerely,

Note to the Author from President Donald J. Trump

POSTSCRIPT

When I felt ready to put all of this together into a book, I had a new problem: finding a publisher who could do it justice. My current publisher did not have the capability to make a color hardbound edition, so I searched around for one…then I realized I already had an ace in my hand, so to speak!

In 2013 I met Jack Gannon, who is co-founder of YBR Publishing, LLC of Ridgeland, South Carolina. He and his partner Cyndi Williams-Barnier were at an authors' conference in Alabama, same as I was, along with many others. After the presentation by Joel Eisenberg, Joel invited everyone to share how they got started. Jack made a presentation of how he and Cyndi got started as authors, and his story touched me so much I had to meet him. That day began a decade-long friendship.

Jack had also been Santa Claus for his hometown of Beaufort, South Carolina, and when he retired from that 23-year career he produced his own memoir, "I Walked In Santa's Boots", a beautiful hardbound book with hundreds of photos from across his Christmas career. That was also the book that launched YBR Publishing in 2016, which has since produced over 30 books, most of them five-star award-winning. I followed Jack and Cyndi as they kept writing their books while publishing multiple genres of books for other authors. After years of witnessing the high-quality books they were producing, I approached them to bring my memoir to print. I knew that they were the ones to bring my story to life.

I signed with YBR in 2021, with the permission of my then-current publisher, to produce a hardbound full-color book of my memoir, which you are holding in your hands today. With Cyndi's husband, Bill, doing the hard editing my manuscript demanded, Cyndi doing follow-up editing, and Jack reviewing everything we had all done as he added the photos and graphics, I wanted my memoir to be formatted and designed to mirror Jack's "Santa" book. Not knowing what the answer would be to that request, I didn't expect him to say, "No problem." He spent eight months designing and refining everything from cover to cover to create this book, with many phone calls and Zoom meetings, to make sure that my discoveries were brought to reality the way I wanted them to look, not the way he thought it should look, with agreements going both ways.

I'd also like to add that in late 2022 YBR announced that it would be producing its first annual anthology, "Tales On the Yellow Brick Road 2023", which was open to anyone wishing to submit short stories and poems. I submitted four stories, and all were approved and accepted for publication, along with several other authors from across the country plus one Canadian poet. This book received an international five-star award.

With the production of this book, and my contract time expired with my previous publisher, I now intend to sign with YBR Publishing for a new series of western novels, with the series name to be "Tales From the True Grit Trail", which pays homage to the Old West marshals out of Fort Smith, plus new stories in "The Gaslight Boys" series.

It's like Jack and Cyndi always say, I apparently traveled my own Yellow Brick Road to get here!

Publisher's Note:

During the pre-production on this memoir in summer 2023, the author provided new computer screen shots that a reasonable person may believe supports what the author has been conveying: that he is the grandson of John Wayne, born Marion Robert Morrison.

The family trees following, provided by The Genealogy Society offices in Paragould, Arkansas and Hopkinsville, Kentucky, allege that the author's father, Billy Gene Hammock, is the son of Marion Robert Morrison (AKA John Wayne) and Lela Pearl Clements.

AN AMERICAN HERITAGE

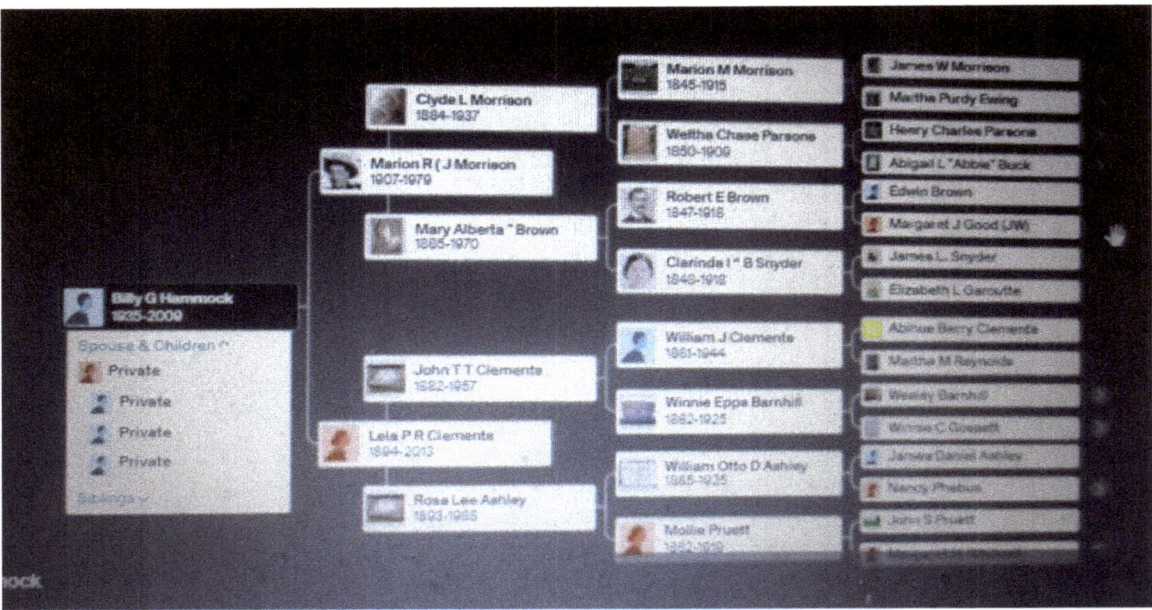

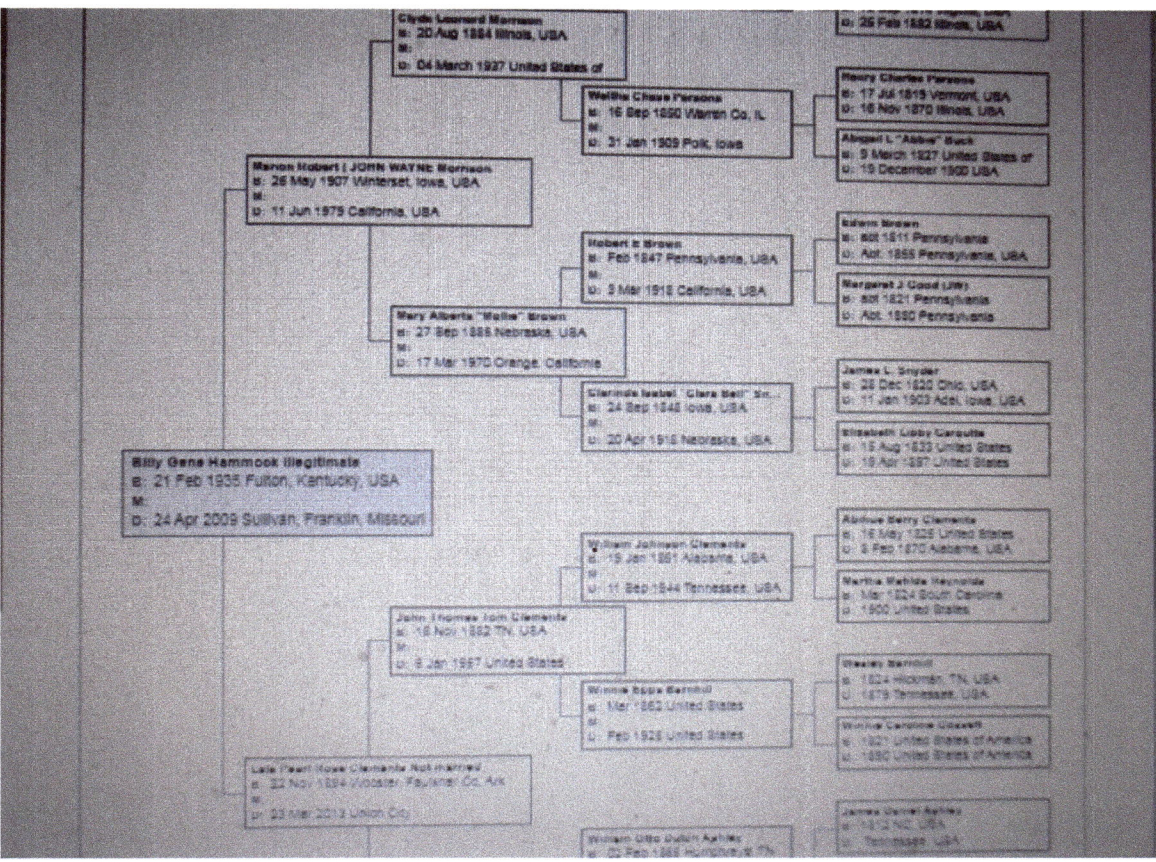

In your opinion, dear reader, does all this lead you to believe that John T. Wayne, born Terry Wayne Hammock to Billy Gene Hammock, who was born to Marion Robert Morrison (John Wayne) and Lela Pearl Clements, is the grandson of John Wayne? Has John T. Wayne (as well as his brothers) finally won his American Heritage? John T. Wayne remains committed to submit a DNA test with any male descendant in John Wayne's family for final verification.

Until then, it ultimately remains for you, the reader, to decide…

ABOUT THE AUTHOR

John T. Wayne is a former marine and truck driver now enjoying retirement and living his dream of being a published author.

A dyslexic since childhood, he survived his school years "by the hair of his chinny-chin-chin". He joined the United States Marine Corps in 1976; after surviving boot camp to become a full Marine, he was appointed as a radio operator. He resigned after six and a half years, married, had two children, and attended the University of Oregon to learn how to write books…until his daughter passed away to cancer. That tragedy ended up resulting in divorce, unfortunately.

When he was writing his first book, "The Treasure del Diablo", he met his future and current wife of 34 years, Donna.

In 2008, his son Ryan passed. Those losses are what drive John forward with his writing, as well as the mission to prove his ancestry, now detailed in this tome.

He was part of the mission to rename an Arkansas highway "The True Grit Trail" with then-Governor Asa Hutchison and continues to help promote it everywhere he travels. He also raises money for the St. Jude Children's Research Hospital in Memphis, Tennessee in his daughter's name, Kimberly Marie.

Today, John stands tall, just as The Duke would have. He hopes his story is shared to everyone, and shares God's Blessings to all.

He and Donna currently live in Corning, Arkansas.

www.ingramcontent.com/pod-product-compliance
Lightning Source LLC
Chambersburg PA
CBHW061407010526
44119CB00011B/281